Framing Africa

Framing Africa

Portrayals of a Continent in Contemporary Mainstream Cinema

Edited by
Nigel Eltringham

berghahn
NEW YORK • OXFORD
www.berghahnbooks.com

Published in 2013 by
Berghahn Books
www.berghahnbooks.com

© 2013 Nigel Eltringham

All rights reserved. Except for the quotation of short passages
for the purposes of criticism and review, no part of this book
may be reproduced in any form or by any means, electronic or
mechanical, including photocopying, recording, or any information
storage and retrieval system now known or to be invented,
without written permission of the publisher.

Library of Congress Cataloging-in-Publication Data
Framing Africa : portrayals of a continent in contemporary mainstream cinema /
edited by Nigel Eltringham.
  pages cm
  Includes bibliographical references and index.
  ISBN 978-1-78238-073-3 (hardback : alk. paper) -- ISBN 978-1-78238-074-0
institutional ebook)
  1. Africa--In motion pictures. 2. Motion pictures--Europe--History--21st century.
  3. Motion pictures--United States--History--21st century. I. Eltringham, Nigel,
editor of compilation.
  PN1995.9.A43F73 2013
  791.43'651--dc23
                                                                   2013006285

British Library Cataloguing in Publication Data
A catalogue record for this book is available from the British Library

Printed in the United States on acid-free paper

ISBN 978-1-78238-073-3 (hardback)
ISBN 978-1-78238-074-0 (ebook)

Contents

Introduction   Cinema/Chimera? The Re-presencing of Africa in Twenty-First-Century Film   1
Nigel Eltringham

One   'Print the Legend': Myth and Reality in *The Last King of Scotland*   21
Mark Leopold

Two   *Black Hawk Down:* Recasting U.S. Military History at Somali Expense   39
Lidwien Kapteijns

Three   Pharma in Africa: Health, Corruption and Contemporary Kenya in *The Constant Gardener*   72
Daniel Branch

Four   War in the City, Crime in the Country: *Blood Diamond* and the Representation of Violence in the Sierra Leone War   91
Danny Hoffman

Five   Showing What Cannot Be Imagined: *Shooting Dogs* and *Hotel Rwanda*   113
Nigel Eltringham

Contents

Six Torture, Betrayal and Forgiveness: *Red Dust* and   135
the Search for Truth in Post-Apartheid South Africa
Annelies Verdoolaege

Seven Go *Amabokoboko!* Rugby, Race, Madiba and   156
the *Invictus* Creation Myth of a New South Africa
Derek Charles Catsam

Notes on Contributors   175

Index   177

Introduction

Cinema/Chimera? The Re-presencing of Africa in Twenty-First-Century Film

Nigel Eltringham

Introduction

In November 2004 I attended the annual meeting of the African Studies Association in New Orleans. A flier inserted into the conference programme invited participants to a screening of a new film, *Hotel Rwanda*, at a small arts cinema nearby. After the showing Terry George, the director, explained that this was a 'low budget' film (U.S.$17 million) that might only get a limited release (at that point there was no U.K. distributor), saying that with a minimal publicity budget, 'We depend on word of mouth to spread the word on this movie'. Three months later the billboard next to my local train station in south London displayed a six-metre-long machete announcing the general release of the film and its three Oscar nominations. The film appeared to have come a long way by word of mouth.

Hotel Rwanda is just one of a series of mainstream North American/European, English-language films set in Africa that were released in the first decade of the new century.[1] In the second half of the previous century one can discern three dominant phases in mainstream, English-speaking, North American/European cinematic portrayals of Africa. First, Africa provided the context for narratives of heroic ascendancy over self (*The African Queen* 1951; *The Snows of Kilimanjaro* 1952), military odds (*Zulu* 1964; *Khartoum* 1966) and nature (*Mogambo* 1953; *Hatari!* 1962; *Born Free* 1966; *The Last Safari* 1967). Attention then turned to retrospective consideration of colonial life, with an emphasis on decay, decadence and race (*Out of Africa* 1985; *White Mischief* 1987). *Cry Freedom* (1987) appeared to herald a different engagement with the continent as the amorphous 'Africa' of recurring exotic caricatures (landscape and wildlife) gave way to the brutal specifics of Apartheid South Africa.[2]

The films considered in this volume can be seen as a new phase, but one in which the cinematic Africa of the 1980s is reversed. Where *Cry Freedom* was an impassioned attempt to educate the world about apartheid, South Africa's story of redemption is now extracted from 'Africa' (*Red Dust* 2004; *Invictus* 2009) while the rest of the continent is no longer a place of romance between Danish baronesses and British big-game hunters (*Out of Africa* 1985), but is blighted by transnational corruption (*The Constant Gardener* 2005), genocide (*Hotel Rwanda* 2004; *Shooting Dogs* 2006), 'failed states' (*Black Hawk Down* 2001), illicit transnational commerce (*Blood Diamond* 2006) and the unfulfilled promises of decolonization (*The Last King of Scotland* 2006). Whereas once Apartheid South Africa (*Cry Freedom* 1987; *A Dry White Season* 1989) was the foil for the romance of East Africa, a redeemed South Africa has now become the foil for violence in the rest of the continent and it is for this reason that *Red Dust* (2004) and *Invictus* (2009) are included in this volume. The same relationship applies to other films that could have been included that promote a redeemed South Africa (*Goodbye Bafana* 2007; *In My Country* 2006) in contrast to rampant violence elsewhere (*Tears of the Sun* 2003; *Sometimes in April* 2005; *Lord of War* 2005; *Darfur* 2009). It is, perhaps, the dominance of the latter theme of violence that explains why no North American/

Introduction

European, mainstream English-language film released since 2000 has been exclusively set in comparatively stable North Africa (pre-Arab Spring and with the exception of Algeria), although segments of films have been set, for example, in Morocco (*Babel* (2006), *The Bourne Ultimatum* (2007), *Hanna* (2011). As regards mainstream Francophone films, only *Des Hommes et des Dieux* (2010) has considered the contemporary situation in Algeria while the most celebrated films, *Indigènes* (2006) and its follow-up *Hors-la-loi* (2010), are historical (set during and in the aftermath of the Second World War) and the action takes place mostly in France.

One of the questions that propels this volume is whether this post-2000 group of films has been able to move away from what Mark Leopold (this volume) describes as the sub-Conradian cliché of Africa as a canvas against which European heroism is enacted. In other words, to what extent do these films continue to engage in the 'distortion of geographical, cultural, human and environmental facts' in order to create a predominantly hostile environment in which a white hero can triumph (Ukadike 1994: 42)? Attention to this reminds us of African cinema and its goal of 'portraying Africa from an African perspective' (Ukadike 1994: 304) through the three broad themes of: 'social realist narratives' that consider current socio-cultural issues; 'colonial confrontation', that puts into conflict Africans and their European colonisers; and 'return to the source', that re-examines pre-colonial African traditions (Diawara 1992: 140–66). Through these different genres, African cinema has been 'struggling to reverse the demeaning portrayals presented by the dominant colonial and commercial cinemas which blatantly distorted African life and culture' (Ukadike 1994: 2; see also Barlet 2000; Gugler 2003; Thackway 2003; Ukadike 2002). Do the films considered here participate in that struggle or do they perpetuate the distortion?

This volume evaluates eight recent films set in Africa by drawing together the views of authors who occupy a particular location. On one hand, they are members of the primary, intended (non-African) audience for these films. But, they are also scholars (historians and

3

anthropologists) with extensive, specialist knowledge of the contexts, events and people portrayed. In the chapters that follow, therefore, the contributors are able to draw on their long-term engagement with specific African contexts to explore the relationship between the film, historical or anthropological knowledge of the context and local perspectives. Further, the contributors reflect on the relation of these films to other contemporary forms of 'Western' knowledge about Africa (news media, documentary, academic commentary and fiction literature) to consider continuities and discontinuities with other portrayals of Africa and Africa's place in the North American/ European imagination.

Africa in the European Imagination

As the contributors note, the writers and directors of the films considered here often express moral motivations. John le Carré considers *The Constant Gardener* as a 'semi-documentary' to expose the activities of pharmaceutical companies in developing countries (Lenzer 2005; see Branch, this volume), while Terry George, director of *Hotel Rwanda*, has stated: 'This story needs to be chronicled, it's one of the greatest acts of heroism of the twentieth century' (Thompson 2005: 52; see Eltringham, this volume). The question remains, however, whether these films (re)produce and perpetuate metaphors and imagined landscapes at odds with the stated intentions of those who write, direct, produce and act in them (Dalby 2008: 443). In other words, do the film scripts reproduce, rather than challenge, a *single* script for 'Africa' which audiences encounter elsewhere in the 'discourse of our times' in which the African experience 'can only be understood through a *negative interpretation*' (Mbembe 2001: 1)? Mark Leopold (this volume) quotes a Ugandan advertising executive commenting on the making of *The Last King of Scotland*: 'You might click your tongue at the perpetuation of the African stereotype of psychotic but disarmingly charming brutes, hopelessly gullible African masses and their obsequiousness towards foreigners, but for now all publicity, any publicity is good'.

Introduction

Whether or not 'any publicity is good publicity', the question is whether Leopold's suggestion regarding *The Last King of Scotland* that 'this is not primarily a film about Ugandan history at all, but a film about Western ideas, or myths, about Africa' could be applied to all eight films? Over the last fifteen years or so political geographers have recognized that film is a form of mapping (or 'cinemato-graphing') in which 'geopolitics is made intelligible and meaningful in the popular realm and through the "everyday"' by (re)producing political and 'moral geographies' and making clear 'the lines of division between "us" and "them"' (Power and Crampton 2005: 195, 198; see Shapiro 1997: 16; Lukinbeal 2004: 247). Alongside other forms of Western media, film produces 'geo-graphs of world politics' which divide the world into 'easy to manage chunks' to make it simple, meaningful and manageable to Western audiences (Sharp 1993: 494; see Dalby 2008: 443).

'Africa' is one such 'easy to manage chunk', not really a place but 'a category through which a "world" is structured' (Ferguson 2006: 5). Neither is 'Africa' as category (rather than place) new. Scholars have detailed the place that 'Africa' (as category) has played in the European/North American imagination (see Comaroff and Comaroff 1991: 86–125; Mudimbe 1988: 16–23; Asad 1973). Described as a 'paradigm of difference' by V.Y. Mudimbe (1994: xii) the alterity ('otherness') of Africa enabled the 'colonial dialectic' (Hardt and Negri 2000: 127) by which Europeans constructed a civilized Self. As Achille Mbembe (2001: 2) writes, 'Africa as an idea, a concept, has historically served, and continues to serve, as a polemical argument for the West's desperate desire to assert its difference from the rest of the world', a sentiment echoed by Chinua Achebe's (1988: 17) observation that 'the West seems to suffer deep anxieties about the precariousness of its civilization and to have a need for a constant reassurance by comparison with Africa'.

Any discussion of cinematic portrayals of 'Africa' (as category) cannot avoid drawing on Edward Said's (2003[1978]) discussion of 'orientalism'. As indicated, 'Africa', like 'the Orient', has 'helped

5

to define Europe (or the West) as its contrasting image, idea, personality, experience' thereby enabling European culture to gain 'in strength and identity'. Ultimately, there is no 'Western civilization' without images of other places including 'Africa' (Said 2003[1978]: 2–3). By describing and representing 'Africa' (including in film) the 'West', it is argued, dominates, restructures and has authority over 'Africa'. Furthermore, as with the image of 'the Orient', Europeans and North Americans enjoy a 'flexible *positioned* superiority' with Africa 'which puts the Westerner in a whole series of relationships ... without ever losing him the relative upper hand' (Said 2003[1978]: 7). Whether it is the romantic Africa of wide savannahs and safari; the compassion-inducing Africa of poverty, disease and famine; or the violent Africa of genocide and torture, the 'Westerner' never loses this 'relative upper hand' of civility because Africa can only be 'pitied, worshipped or dominated' (Wainaina 2005). If this 'flexible *positioned* superiority' is integral to representations of 'Africa', the question remains of whether it can be overcome in films which, on the surface, denounce relationships of superiority/exploitation, whether by pharmaceutical companies (*The Constant Gardener*); dealers in illicit diamonds (*Blood Diamond*); or distant, disinterested politicians (*Hotel Rwanda; Shooting Dogs*)?

What unites the films considered here is that they are all concerned with subjects of which a European/North American audience will already possess some awareness through 'factual' news media. The realist illusion, that films are 'no more than a window onto unmediated "reality"' (Rosenstone 1992: 507) is, therefore, accentuated, drawing upon an audience's (deceptive) sense of familiarity and recognition. As many scholars have demonstrated, news media coverage of 'Africa' in North American and Europe is overwhelmingly negative (Ebo 1992; Brookes 1995; Hachten and Beil 1985; Hickey and Wylie 1993; McCarthy 1983; Schraeder and Endless 1998; Zein and Cooper 1992). As Beverley Hawk (1992: 6) states in the introduction to her seminal edited volume, the common theme of media coverage of 'Africa' is that 'Africa is a failure and needs our help'. It has been noted that a distinct language/script is employed to describe 'Africa'. For example, while the English-speaking press described the Bosnian conflict as political and ethnic and employed the 'language of civil war' (involving 'strategies' and 'leaders'), the concurrent 1994 Rwandan genocide was described as 'timeless' and 'tribal' and employed the 'language of savagery' (such as 'bloodthirsty' and 'orgy') (Myers, Klak, and Koehl 1996: 29; see Allen and Seaton 1999; Alozie 2007; Eltringham 2004: 63–8; Livingston 2007; Wall 1997a, 1997b). In other words, African conflicts were described using a 'different vocabulary' from those in Europe because, it has been argued, 'African events do not follow any pattern recognisable to Western reason' (see Hawk 1992: 7). In so doing, the news media perpetuates the 'moral epistemology of imperialism' (Said 1993: 18) because 'without such encounters, the West would not know its own civility' (Razack 2003: 208).

Scholars have also noted a tendency of 'geo-conflation' in news media coverage of Africa in which the latest crisis in one part of the continent is 'extrapolated to an undifferentiated continental ruin' (Myers, Klak, and Koehl 1996: 38; see Wainaina 2005). While Africans in films made in the first half of the twentieth century all spoke Swahili and lived in one landscape (East Africa) (Cameron 1994: 12), today, South Africa stands in for Rwanda (*Hotel Rwanda*); Morocco for Somalia (*Black Hawk Down*); and Mozambique and South Africa for Sierra Leone (*Blood Diamond*). This results in 'a composite Africa [which] does little to disrupt or challenge most of the films' audience, for whom Africa is a singular and largely un-nuanced unit' (Hoffman, this volume). The transformation of particular episodes into placeless archetypes finds another expression in the way 'Africans' are invariably represented as an anonymized 'frantic mass' rather than specific persons with 'a name, opinions, relatives, and histories' (Malkki 1996: 387–89; see Wainaina 2005 Eltringham and Kapteijns this volume).[3] Such portrayals of 'Africa', Beverly Hawk (1992: 13) has argued, means that European and North American audiences 'do not really get any news from Africa', only repetitive images that 'correspond to notions about Africa already existent in the minds of Westerners'. Just as eighteenth- and nineteenth-century African travelogues simply brought 'new proofs' of 'African inferiority' already established in the European imagination (Mudimbe 1988: 13), so contemporary news media reports are simply reiterations of well-established themes.

Although research suggests that media coverage of Africa may be moving away from being predominantly negative (see Scott 2009; Kothari 2010), when the films considered here allude to news media it is to the *negative* media coverage of 'Africa'. In *Hotel Rwanda*, for example, the TV journalist David excitedly tells his editor on the phone: 'I've got incredible footage. It's a massacre, dead bodies, machetes. If I get this through right away can you make the evening news?' In *Shooting Dogs* Joe Conner asks Christopher if he can bring a BBC TV crew to the school in which they are besieged, arguing that 'Nowadays, nothing exists if it's not on TV'. In *Black Hawk Down*, when a colleague asks Staff Sergeant Matt Eversmann whether he likes Somalis, he replies, 'We have two things that we can do. We can either help or we can sit back and watch the country destroy itself on CNN'. And in *Blood Diamond* the magazine journalist, Maddy, takes a series of archetypal, Sebastião Salgadoesque, black and white photos of refugees and later declares, 'It's like one of those infomercials with little black babies with swollen bellies and flies in their eyes. Except here I've got dead mothers; I've got severed limbs, but it's nothing new ... I'm sick of writing about victims, but it's all I fucking do'. The paradox is, of course, that these moments in which the news media is challenged for stereotyping Africa as a place of violence is done within films that take violence in Africa as their subject with the dramatic opportunities that entails.

The influence of the news media on these films, however, goes beyond these explicit allusions. One of Said's insights is how portrayals of 'the Orient' acquire 'mass and density, and referential power among themselves and thereafter in the culture at large' (Said 2003[1978]: 20). For Said, *all* representations of 'the Orient' are his subject of study, whether written by scholars, fiction authors, travel writers or journalists. They possess this unity because 'they frequently refer to each other' (Said 2003[1978]: 23). The same can be said of cinematic and news media portrayals of 'Africa'. In the films considered here there are explicit instances of such self-reference between news media and cinematic portrayal. A number of films use VOA or BBC world service radio broadcasts to provide 'context' (*Hotel Rwanda*; *Blood Diamond*) and *Shooting Dogs* ends with the footage of the infamous State Department press conference on 28 April 1994 at which the official refused to call events in Rwanda 'genocide'. What is more striking, however, is that a number of the films restage news media footage: footage of Rwandan Tutsi being killed (*Hotel Rwanda*); Nelson Mandela's release (*Invictus*); Somalis fighting over a food delivery at a Red Cross Food Distribution Centre (*Black Hawk Down*); an exhumation carried out by investigators for the South African Truth and Reconciliation Commission (*Red Dust*); or, in the case of *The Last King of Scotland*, scenes 'copied frame for frame' from a documentary (see Leopold, this volume). As Danny Hoffman (this volume) observes of the restaging of the 1999 attack on Freetown by the Revolutionary United Front in *Blood Diamond*:

> Much of this sequence is shot with hand held, mobile cameras. Zwick [the director] describes his desire in this scene in particular to capture the aesthetic of documentary films from the period, many of which were shot on small cameras from hidden positions ... To enhance the newsreel effect, in at least some of these scenes the camera operators were not told how the action would unfold, leaving them to shoot as though they were photojournalists documenting unscripted news.

The use or restaging of news media images in these films suggest that anyone who represents 'Africa' assumes some precedent, some previous knowledge 'to which he refers and on which he relies' so that the representation '*affiliates* itself with other works' (Said 2003[1978]: 20). In other words, fictional(ized) stories about Africa 'pick up on other media, either resonating with or amplifying the already known' (Sharp 1996: 158). Such restaging and the evident self-reference between the news media and films raises the question of how far these films can move from the negative *scripts* of news media coverage of 'Africa' (see Sharp 1996: 159).

The anonymous, 'frantic mass' (Malkki 1996: 387–89) so often portrayed in news media coverage of Africa remains evident in these films. As Lidwien Kapteijns (this volume) observes of *Black Hawk Down*, 'The film's rendering of the Somalis as an undifferentiated, generically Black, violent mob is a strategy that creates enormous moral distance between them and the film's audience'. On the other hand, a number of the films self-consciously comment on empathy, perhaps in an attempt to counter news media portrayal and bring individual Africans within the audience's 'universe of moral obligation' (Fein 1993: 43). Challenges to the audience's assumed inability to empathize with Africans are made in *Shooting Dogs* when Rachel, a BBC journalist confesses, 'Anytime I saw a dead Bosnian woman, a white woman, I thought ... that could be my mum. Over here they're just dead Africans', and in *Hotel Rwanda* when Jack, a TV cameraman says, 'I think if people see this footage they'll say, "Oh my God that's horrible," and then go on eating their dinners'. In *Blood Diamond*, when asked to help the Sierra Leonean Solomon, the magazine journalist Maddy responds, 'Why? This whole country is at war. Why should I just help one person? [pause] I can't believe I just said that'. The attempt to personalize the 'frantic mass' and challenge the limits of audience empathy is also found in *The Constant Gardener* in the following exchange between Justin, a British diplomat, and Jonah, a UN pilot as they flee a Sudanese refugee camp under attack by 'tribesmen':

Jonah: I'm sorry. I can't take the girl.
Justin: I'm not leaving her.
Jonah: We're only allowed to evacuate aid workers.
Justin: Well, to hell with what's allowed. I'll ... How much do you want for her? Look, there's $800.
Jonah: Look, don't embarrass me. You can't buy this. The rules are made for good reason.
Justin: This is a child's life! There are no rules to cover that!
Jonah: Look, there are thousands of them out there. I can't make an exception for this one child.

Introduction

Justin: But this is one we can help, here!
Jonah: Listen, that's the way it is here. Keep your money. Strap yourself in, and let's go.

These self-conscious reflections on moral responsibility also draw attention to the fact that in a number of films the key characters are non-African: Joe Conner in *Shooting Dogs*, Nicholas Garrigan in *The Last King of Scotland* and Justin Quayle in *The Constant Gardener*. On one hand, this is an example of Achille Mbembe's (Mbembe 2001: 3) observation that 'narrative about Africa is always a pretext for a comment about something else, some other place, some other people'. Africa becomes simply a backdrop for exemplars of the naïve gap year student (*Shooting Dogs; The Last King of Scotland*); the alienated diplomat (*The Constant Gardener*); the reformed mercenary (*Blood Diamond*). And yet, when directors argue that their films are designed to 'educate' a non-African audience, these 'outsiders' are a pedagogical device who, as audience surrogates, can engage in 'informative dialogues' (Duage-Roth 2010: 196) and revelatory journeys that enlighten the equally 'outsider' audience. As Michael Caton-Jones, director of *Shooting Dogs*, has argued, 'It's told through the eyes of westerners because there is no point telling the Rwandans. They know what happened. My job is to tell the story to the west so that they will understand' (Walker 2004). Although persuasive, employing the 'innocent abroad' device risks reproducing the impressionistic, sensationalist spectatorship of the colonial travelogue (see Basaninyenzi 2006) or the 'heroic figure of the white man rescuing the African' (Duage-Roth 2010: 183). As Mark Leopold (this volume) observes of *The Last King of Scotland*, 'placing a white character at the centre of the narrative tends to reduce the film to the standard sub-Conradian cliché of Africa as a blank contrast to European heroism' (see also Hoffman, this volume). Then again, to assume that African lead characters would be intrinsically more 'authentic' reproduces the illusion of the realist film which obscures the fact that nothing within its frame(s) is actually 'authentic' or 'true'.

Veracity and Invention

The question of 'truth' is pertinent given that, with the exception of *The Constant Gardener*, all of the films considered in this volume are realist portrayals of 'historical' events.[4] For many in the audience these films will be their sole history lesson on a particular event/ context. As Derek Catsam (this volume) states in relation to *Invictus* (2009), 'as with most films depicting historical events, people probably should not learn their history from *Invictus*, but huge numbers of people will'. There is a need, therefore, to consider their historical veracity. It is argued that the ideological power of cinema derives from 'creating an illusion that what happens on screen is a neutral recording of objective events, rather than a construct operating from a certain point of view' (Ryan and Kellner 1988: 1). The insinuation here is that other representations (including those produced by the historian or anthropologist) are, somehow, not constructed from a 'certain point of view'. It is instructive that Catherine Njeri Ngugi (2003: 58) begins her critical comparison of Ousame Sembène's *Camp de Tharoye* (1988) and Richard Attenborough's *Cry Freedom* (1987) with the historian E.H. Carr's (1987: 11) observation; 'It used to be said that facts speak for themselves. This is, of course, untrue. The facts speak only when the historian calls on them: it is he who decides to which facts to give the floor, and in what order or context'. For the historian, anthropologist or filmmaker, therefore, 'there is no such thing as a delivered presence, but a *re-presence*, or a representation' (Said 2003[1978]: 21).

To argue that unlike written history (and by extension anthropology), a realist historical film is arbitrary and selective, and thus deceptive, is to misconstrue written history. Written history is not simply 'an organised compilation of facts', for '"facts" never stand alone but are always called forth (or constituted) by the work in which they then become embedded' (Rosenstone 1992: 506). Just as a film is not a simple transference of scholarly history to the screen, so written history is not a simple transference of the past into written form (see Browning 1992; White 1987). We must be alert to the fact that while cinematic history is not written history, neither is written history unmediated facts but a 'construction' (Worden 2007: 87; see Eltringham 2004: 147–60). These films are also constructions and, as a consequence, we should not judge them according to a 'literalist mimetic mode' (Dalby 2008: 450). The recognition that neither history nor film employs a 'literalist mimetic mode' must influence the ways these films are assessed. Derek Catsam (this volume), for example, discussing the attempt in *Invictus* to bring the complexities of post-apartheid South Africa to an audience that knows little about the country's history, concedes: 'It would be easy to dismiss such efforts from the perch of academia but in this case surely half a loaf is better than none at all'. In fact, it can be argued that by deviating from a 'literalist mimetic mode' realist films (including those considered here) may deliver greater 'veracity'. Regarding *The Last King of Scotland*, Mark Leopold (this volume) suggests that in the case of Idi Amin 'myths or legends may be truer to the realities of life than a pure recitation of fully confirmed facts' and that to assess the film 'solely on matters of fact would be to miss the film's ability to capture the metaphorical reality of his rule that continues to haunt contemporary Uganda and inform Western imageries of Africa'. Robert Rosentsone (2000: 62) makes related observations, that 'film will always include images that are at once invented and true; true in that they symbolize, condense, or summarize larger amounts of data; true in that they impart an overall meaning of the past that can be verified, documented or reasonably argued'. Such abbreviation is required for a plausible dramatic structure and necessary if the film is to communicate with a diverse audience (Toplin 1996: 5). It is not, therefore, 'invention' per se which is the problem (compression, condensation, alteration or metaphor which still remains true to a wider knowledge of the contexts portrayed), but 'false' invention, which chooses to ignore that wider knowledge (Rosenstone 2000: 62–4). We need to ask, therefore, whether the films considered here 'ignore the findings and assertions and arguments of what we already know from other sources' (Rosenstone 2000: 62) or do they contain 'impressively imaginative efforts to speak the truth through mythic images' (Toplin 1996: 13)? An example of a 'true invention' would be the fact that although there has not been a pharmaceutical scandal in Kenya of the kind portrayed in *The Constant Gardener*, Daniel Branch (this volume) indicates that there have been analogous events in West Africa.

One of the 'true inventions' that realist films engage in, but which is rarely acknowledged, is to make the audience into eye-witnesses to what is attested to in other sources but of which there is no footage. In our hyper-mediatized world it is easy to forget that we do not have footage of the South African police or Idi Amin torturing people (*Red Dust; Last King of Scotland*). And yet, because the realist film 'abhors a vacuum; it converts the absence of the past into a visible presence' (Hirsch 2004: 21). This is, perhaps, most clear in *Red Dust*. Annelies Verdoolaege (this volume) discusses how South African special branch policeman Jeffrey Benzien re-enacted the 'wet bag' torture method in front of the South African Truth and Reconciliation Commission. In *Red Dust* the 'tools' of torture are also brought to the hearing for the Commissioner's to inspect, but Benzien's 'safe' re-enactment with an unharmed volunteer is replaced with a flashback exposing the audience to the true horror.

Ultimately, the 'meanings, messages and connotations' of the films considered here are 'constructed differently depending on who is viewing and where they are viewing from' (Lisle and Pepper 2005: 169). Each of the contributors responds to their film from their own particular location. Underpinning their assessments is a tension: the desire for greater knowledge and understanding of Africa, but recognition of the great obstacles that lie in the way. As Kenneth Cameron (1994: 13) observes:

> When the filmic 'Africa' and the Africa are compared, a disjunction can always be found. Some of this disjunction is the result of ignorance, some of indifference, some of willful blindness, some of governmental or industrial interference or even censorship; but some of it is inevitable – the impossibility of ever capturing an almost infinite complexity with the camera.

Introduction

Notes

1. For reflection on pre-2000 films see Bickford-Smith and Mendelsohn (2007).
2. For a more detailed discussion of cinematic 'Africa' in the twentieth century see Cameron (1994).
3. Liisa Malkki (1996: 388) notes the prevalence of women and children in depictions of refugees, denoting a 'certain kind of helplessness' (see also Burman 1994).
4. Although portraying historical events, *Red Dust* is an adaptation of a novel (Slovo 2000).

Filmography

Attenborough, R. (Dir.) 1987. *Cry Freedom* (Universal Pictures, Marble Arch Productions).
August, B. (Dir.) 2007. *Goodbye Bafana* (Banana Films, Arsam International, Film Afrika Worldwide, Future Films, Thema Production, X-Filme Creative Pool).
Beauvois, X. (Dir.) 2010. *Des Hommes et des Dieux* (Why Not Productions, Armada Films, France 3 Cinéma).
Boll, U. (Dir.) 2009. *Darfur* (Event Film Distribution, Pitchblack Pictures Inc., ZenHQ Films).
Boorman, J. (Dir.) 2006. *In My Country* (Chartoff Productions, Film Afrika Worldwide, Film Consortium, Industrial Development Corporation of South Africa, Merlin Films, Phoenix Pictures, Studio Eight Productions, U.K. Film Council).
Bouchareb, R. (Dir.) 2006. *Indigènes* (Tessalit Productions).
_____. (Dir.) 2010. *Hors-la-loi* (Tessalit Productions).
Caton-Jones, M. (Dir.) 2005. *Shooting Dogs* (CrossDay Productions Ltd., ARTE, BBC Films, Egoli Tossell Film, Filmstiftung Nordrhein-Westfalen, Invicta Capital, U.K. Film Council, Zweites Deutsches Fernsehen (ZDF)).
Dearden, B. (Dir.) 1966. *Khartoum* (Julian Blaustein Productions Ltd.).
Eastwood, C. (Dir.) 2009. *Invictus* (Warner Bros. Pictures, Spyglass Entertainment, Revelations Entertainment, Mace Neufeld Productions, Malpaso Productions).
Endfield, C. (Dir.) 1964. *Zulu* (Diamond Films).
Ford, J. (Dir.) 1953. *Mogambo* (Loew's).
Fuqua, A. (Dir.) 2003. *Tears of the Sun* (Cheyenne Enterprises, Michael Lobell Productions, Revolution Studios).
George, T. (Dir.) 2004. *Hotel Rwanda* (United Artists).
Greengrass, P. (Dir.) 2007 *The Bourne Ultimatum* (Universal Pictures, Kennedy/Marshall Company, Kanzaman, Angel Studios, Ludlum Entertainment, Motion Picture BETA Produktionsgesellschaft)

15

Hathaway, H. (Dir.) 1967. *The Last Safari* (Paramount Pictures).
Hawks, H. (Dir.) 1962. *Hatari!* (Malabar).
Hill, J. (Dir.) 1966. *Born Free* (Columbia Pictures Corporation, Open Road Films, Atlas Films Ltd.).
Hooper, T. (Dir.) 2004. *Red Dust* (British Broadcasting Corporation, Distant Horizon, Videovision Entertainment, Industrial Development Corporation of South Africa, BBC Films).
Huston, J. (Dir.) 1951. *The African Queen* (Romulus Films, Horizon Pictures).
Iñárritu, A. G. (Dir.), 2006 *Babel* (Zeta Film, Anonymous Content, Paramount Pictures, Central Films, Paramount Vantage, Media Rights Capital).
King, H. (Dir.) 1952. *The Snows of Kilimanjaro* (Twentieth Century Fox Film Corporation).
Macdonald, K. (Dir.) 2006. *The Last King of Scotland* (Fox Searchlight Pictures, DNA Films, FilmFour, U.K. Film Council, Scottish Screen, Cowboy Films, Slate Films, Tatfilm).
Meirelles, F. (Dir.) 2005. *The Constant Gardener* (Focus Features, Potboiler Productions).
Niccol, A. (Dir.) 2005. *Lord of War* (Entertainment Manufacturing Company, VIP 3 Medienfonds, Ascendant Pictures, Saturn Films, Rising Star, Copag V, Endgame Entertainment).
Palcy, E. (Dir.) 1989. *A Dry White Season* (Davros Films Star Partners II Ltd., Sundance Productions).
Peck, R. (Dir.) 2005. *Sometimes in April* (CINEFACTO, HBO Films, Velvet Film).
Pollack, S. (Dir.) 1985. *Out of Africa* (Mirage Enterprises, Universal Pictures).
Radford, M. (Dir.) 1987. *White Mischief* (Goldcrest Films International, Nelson Entertainment, Power Tower Investments, Umbrella Films).
Scott, R. (Dir.) 2001. *Black Hawk Down* (Revolution Studios, Jerry Bruckheimer Films).
Sembene, O. (Dir.) 1988. *Camp de Tharoye* (Enaproc, Films Domireew, Films Kajoor, Satpec, Société Nouvelle Pathé Cinéma).
Wright, J. (Dir.), 2011 *Hanna* (Focus Features, Studio Babelsberg, Holleran Company).
Zwick, E. (Dir.) 2006. *Blood Diamond* (Warner Bros. Pictures, Virtual Studios, Spring Creek Productions, Bedford Falls Productions, Lonely Film Productions GmbH & Co. KG.).

References

Achebe, C. 1988. *Hopes and Impediments: Selected Essays, 1965–1987*. London: Doubleday.

Introduction

Allen, T. and J. Seaton (eds). 1999. *The Media of Conflict: War Reporting and Representations of Ethnic Violence*. London: Zed.
Alozie, E. 2007. 'What Did They Say? African Media Coverage of the First 100 Days of the Rwanda Crisis', in A. Thompson (ed.), *The Media and the Rwanda Genocide*. London: Pluto Press, pp. 211–31.
Asad, T. 1973. 'Two European Images of Non-European Rule', *Economy and Society* 2(3): 263–77.
Barlet, O. 2000. *African Cinemas: Decolonising the Gaze*. London: Zed.
Basaninyenzi, G. 2006. '"Dark Faced Europeans": The Nineteenth Century Colonial Travelogue and the Invention of the Hima Race', in J. Young and J.E. Braziel (eds), *Race and the Foundations of Knowledge: Cultural Amnesia in the Academy*. University of Illinois Press, pp. 114–26.
Bickford-Smith, V. and R. Mendelsohn (eds). 2007. *Black and White in Colour: African History on Screen*. Oxford: James Currey.
Brookes, H. 1995. 'Suit, Tie and a Touch of Juju – The Ideological Construction of Africa: A Critical Discourse Analysis of News on Africa in the British Press', *Discourse and Society* 6(4): 461–94.
Browning, C. 1992. 'German Memory, Judicial Interrogation, and Historical Reconstruction: Writing Perpetrator History from Postwar Testimony', in S. Friedländer (ed.), *Probing the Limits of Representation: Nazism and the 'Final Solution'*. Cambridge, MA: Harvard University Press, pp. 22–36.
Burman, E. 1994. 'Innocents Abroad: Western Fantasies of Childhood and the Iconography of Emergencies', *Disasters* 18(3): 238–53.
Cameron, K.M. 1994. *Africa on Film: Beyond Black and White*. New York: Continuum.
Carr, E.H. 1987. *What is History?* 2nd ed. London: Penguin.
Comaroff, J. and J. Comaroff. 1991. *Of Revelation and Revolution*. Chicago: University of Chicago Press.
Dalby, S. 2008. 'Warrior Geopolitics: Gladiator, Black Hawk Down and The Kingdom of Heaven', *Political Geography* 27(4): 439–55.
Diawara, M. 1992. *African Cinema: Politics and Culture*. Bloomington: Indiana University Press.
Duage-Roth, A. 2010. *Writing and Filming the Genocide of the Tutsis in Rwanda: Dismembering and Remembering Traumatic History*. Lanham, MD: Lexington Books.
Ebo, B. 1992. 'American Media and African Culture', in B.G. Hawk (ed.), *Africa's Media Image*. New York: Praeger, pp. 15–25.
Eltringham, N. 2004. *Accounting for Horror: Post-Genocide Debates in Rwanda*. London: Pluto.
Fein, H. 1993. *Genocide: A Sociological Perspective*. London: Sage.
Ferguson, J. 2006. *Global Shadows: Africa in the Neoliberal World Order*. Durham, NC: Duke University Press.
Gugler, J. 2003. *African Film: Re-imagining a Continent*. Oxford: James Currey.

Hachten, W. and B. Beil. 1985. 'Bad News or No News?': Covering Africa 1965–1982', *Journalism Quarterly* 62(3): 626–30.
Hardt, M. and A. Negri. 2000. *Empire*. Cambridge, MA: Harvard University Press.
Hawk, B. 1992. 'Introduction: Metaphors of African Coverage', in B. Hawk (ed.), *Africa's Media Image*. New York: Praeger Publishers, pp. 3–14.
Hickey, D., and K. Wylie. 1993. *An Enchanting Darkness: The American Vision of Africa in the Twentieth Century*. East Lansing: Michigan State University Press.
Hirsch, J.F. 2004. *Afterimage: Film, Trauma, and the Holocaust. Emerging Media*. Philadelphia: Temple University Press.
Kothari, A. 2010. 'The Framing of the Darfur Conflict in the New York Times: 2003–2006', *Journalism Studies* 11(2): 209–24.
Lenzer, J. 2005. 'The Constant Gardener', *British Medical Journal* 331(7514): 462.
Lisle, D. and A. Pepper. 2005. 'The New Face of Global Hollywood: Black Hawk Down and the Politics of Meta-Sovereignty', *Cultural Politics: An International Journal* 1(2): 165–92.
Livingston, S. 2007. 'Limited Vision: How Both the American Media and Government Failed Rwanda', in A. Thompson (ed.), *The Media and the Rwanda Genocide*. London: Pluto Press, pp. 188–97.
Lukinbeal, C. 2004. 'The Map that Precedes the Territory: An Introduction to Essays in Cinematic Geography', *GeoJournal* 59(4): 247–51.
Malkki, L.H. 1996. 'Speechless Emissaries: Refugees, Humanitarianism, and Dehistoricization', *Cultural Anthropology* 11(3): 377–404.
Mbembe, J.A. 2001. *On the Postcolony*. Berkeley, CA: University of California Press.
McCarthy, M. 1983. *Dark Continent: Africa as Seen by Americans*. Westport: Greenwood Press.
Mudimbe, V.Y. 1988. *The Invention of Africa: Gnosis, Philosophy, and the Order of Knowledge*. Oxford: James Currey.
_____. 1994. *The Idea of Africa*. Bloomington, IN: Indiana University Press.
Myers, G., T. Klak and T. Koehl. 1996. 'The Inscription of Difference: News Coverage of the Conflicts in Rwanda and Burundi', *Political Geography* 15(1): 21–46.
Ngugi, N. 2003. 'Presenting and (Mis)representing History in Fiction Film: Sembène's "Camp de Thiaroye" and Attenborough's "Cry Freedom"', *Journal of African Cultural Studies* 16(1): 57–68.
Power, M. and A. Crampton. 2005. 'Reel Politics: Cinemato-graphing Political Space', *Geopolitics* 10(2): 193–203.
Razack, S. 2003. 'Those Who "Witness the Evil"', *Hypatia* 18(1): 204–11.
Rosenstone, R.A. 1992. 'JFK: Historical Fact/Historical Film', *The American Historical Review* 97(2): 506–11.

———. 2000. 'The Historical Film: Looking at the Past in a Postliterate Age', in M. Landy (ed.), *The Historical Film: History and Memory in Media*. New Brunswick, NJ: Rutgers University Press, pp. 50–66.

Ryan, M. and D. Kellner. 1988. *Camera Politica: The Politics and Ideology of Contemporary Hollywood Film*. Bloomington Indiana: Indiana University Press.

Said, E. 1993. *Culture and Imperialism*. New York: Alfred A. Knopf.

———. 2003[1978]. *Orientalism*. London: Penguin.

Schraeder, P.J. and B. Endless. 1998. 'The Media and Africa: The Portrayal of Africa in the "New York Times" (1955–1995)', *Issue: A Journal of Opinion* 26(2): 29–35.

Scott, M. 2009. 'Marginalized, Negative or Trivial? Coverage of Africa in the UK Press', *Media, Culture and Society* 31(4): 533–57.

Shapiro, M.J. 1997. *Violent Cartographies: Mapping Cultures of War*. Minneapolis, MN; London: University of Minnesota Press.

Sharp, J. 1996. 'Reel Geographies of the New World Order', in G.O. Tuathail and S. Dalby (eds). *Rethinking Geopolitics*. London: Routledge, pp. 152–69.

Sharp, J.P. 1993. 'Publishing American identity: popular geopolitics, myth and The Reader's Digest', *Political Geography* 12(6): 491–503.

Slovo, G. 2000. *Red Dust*. London: Virago Press.

Thackway, M. 2003. *Africa Shoots Back: Alternative Perspectives in Sub-Saharan Francophone African Film*. Oxford: James Currey.

Thompson, A. 2005. 'The Struggle of Memory against Forgetting', in T. George (ed.), *Hotel Rwanda: Bringing the True Story of an African Hero to Film*. New York: Newmarket Press, pp. 47–59.

Toplin, R.B. 1996. *History by Hollywood: The Use and Abuse of the American Past*. Urbana: University of Illinois Press.

Ukadike, N.F. 1994. *Black African Cinema*. Berkeley CA: University of California Press.

———. 2002. *Questioning African Cinema: Conversations with Filmmakers*. Minneapolis, MN: University of Minnesota Press.

Wainaina, B. 2005. 'How to write about Africa', *Granta* 92. Retrieved 1 November 2011 from http://www.granta.com/Archive/92/How-to-Write-about-Africa/Page-1

Walker, R. 2004. 'Bringing Genocide to the Big Screen', *BBC News*, 2 August 2004. Retrieved 1 November 2011 from http://news.bbc.co.uk/1/hi/entertainment/3527130.stm

Wall, M.A. 1997a. 'A "Pernicious New Strain of the Old Nazi Virus" and an "Orgy of Tribal Slaughter": A Comparison of US News Magazine Coverage of the Crisis in Bosnia and Rwanda', *Gazette* 59(6): 411–28.

———. 1997b. 'The Rwanda Crisis: An Analysis of News Magazine Coverage', *Gazette* 59(2): 121–34.

White, H.V. 1987. *The Content of the Form: Narrative Discourse and Historical Representation*. Baltimore: Johns Hopkins University Press.
Worden, N. 2007. 'What Are We?": *Proteus* and the Problematising of History', in V. Bickford-Smith and R. Mendelsohn (eds), *Black and White in Colour: African History on Screen*. Oxford: James Currey, pp. 82–96.
Zein, H.M., and A. Cooper. 1992. '*New York Times* Coverage of Africa', in B.G. Hawk (ed.), *Africa's Media Image*. New York: Praeger, pp. 121–32.

One

'Print the Legend'
Myth and Reality in *The Last King of Scotland*

Mark Leopold

> 'This is the West, sir. When the legend becomes fact, print the legend,' said by the Editor of the *Shinbone Star* newspaper, in *The Man Who Shot Liberty Valance* (Dir. John Ford, 1962).[1]

The main characteristic of *The Last King of Scotland*, Kevin Macdonald's 2006 film about Idi Amin Dada (President of Uganda from 1971 to 1979), is its air of verisimilitude. Students and others with whom I have discussed the film invariably ask whether it is true, and some are shocked when I point out that it is a work of fiction, based on Giles Foden's 1998 novel of the same name. A cursory internet search of the film title reveals a similar obsession with its truthfulness or lack thereof. The Wikipedia entry, for example, (accessed 28 September 2011) includes a section headed 'Historical accuracy', which states that:

> [w]hile the character of Idi Amin and the events surrounding him in the movie are mostly factual, Garrigan is a fictional character ... Like the novel on which it is based, the film mixes fiction with real events in Ugandan history to give an impression of Amin and Uganda under his

authoritarian rule. While the basic events of Amin's life are followed, the film often departs from actual history in the details of particular events.

Questions of truth take on a particular quality given that *The Last King of Scotland* was Macdonald's first fictional film, after an earlier career as a documentary filmmaker,[2] and that the film restages scenes from Barbet Schroeder's 1974 documentary *General Idi Amin Dada (A Self Portrait)*. Macdonald's attitude to the relationship between truth and fiction, surely informed by his earlier career, is apparent in his commentary on the DVD version of the film. Macdonald makes it clear that he is concerned with the truth of the film and its faithfulness to the historical facts about Amin's rule. In this commentary Macdonald repeatedly refers to the number of 'real' items and scenes he used. His comments include: 'That tracksuit is really based on a tracksuit he used to wear'; 'This scene is actually based on a documentary by Barbet Schroeder'; 'That's the real chair Amin used to sit on at the head of the Cabinet'; 'That's Amin's real helicopter, the presidential helicopter'. While fully aware that the story is fiction, his aim was clearly to make the film as real as possible. And there is much that is truthful about *The Last King of Scotland*, especially Forest Whitaker's magnificent performance in the title role. Whitaker even catches Amin's West Nile accent perfectly (which is distinct, for example, from a southern Ugandan accent). Nevertheless, I will argue here that whatever its factual status, the film remains faithful to the mythical status that Amin has attained. I will also suggest, therefore, that to assess the film solely on matters of fact would be to miss the film's ability to capture the metaphorical reality of his rule that continues to haunt contemporary Uganda and inform Western imageries of Africa.

The plot begins with a young Scottish doctor, Nicholas Garrigan (James McAvoy), looking for a post-graduation African adventure. Choosing Uganda at random, he arrives to become instantly captivated by the beauty of the land and, determined to 'make a difference', he takes up a post at a Ugandan hospital. Again by chance he attends a rally held by the country's new leader, Idi Amin Dada

Myth and Reality in The Last King of Scotland

(Forest Whitaker), and is swept away by Amin's charismatic personality. Amin notices his enthusiasm and, after initially threatening him, learns Garrigan is Scottish. Being fond of the Scots, the President takes the young man under his wing, asking him to become his personal physician. Garrigan attends a series of occasions at which Amin alternately jokes with, bullies, and threatens his Cabinet and other colleagues, demonstrating as he does his physical prowess and manipulative skills. The doctor also goes to wild parties thrown by the dictator, at which he meets and falls for Amin's youngest wife, Kay (Kerry Washington). Despite being warned, and shown corpses, by a cynical English diplomat, Stone (Simon McBurney), and a Ugandan medical colleague, Dr Junju (David Oyelowu), Garrigan does his best to avoid recognizing, or accepting the fact of, the rising number of atrocities being committed by Amin's supporters. Events spiral out of control. The mass killings increase, Garrigan sleeps with Kay and she becomes pregnant. He clashes with Amin's security chiefs and argues with the dictator himself. Then (as happened in fact) an Air France plane from Tel Aviv is hijacked by Palestinian guerrillas and flown to Uganda. The cast (minus Kay, who has been killed) are all at the airport. Amin tells Garrigan that he knows about Kay and has him tortured. As Israeli guerrillas arrive to free the hostages, the security people leave Garrigan hanging from meat hooks. He is rescued by Dr Junju and put on the plane flying the hostages out. The film ends with a brief résumé of events and some documentary photographs of Amin.

In Uganda itself, the film aroused considerable interest and excitement. Few films had been made in the country, and no Hollywood blockbusters. South Africa or Kenya usually represent 'Africa' for filmmakers (see Introduction and Hoffman, this volume), and perhaps offer more familiar comforts to the actors and crew. The Ugandan government was supportive: its official press emphasized the jobs created by the film – for actors (including up to 6,000 extras, many from the Ugandan army), dressmakers, electricians and other trades – and for its potential impact on tourism revenue.[3] Uganda's President, Yoweri Museveni, appointed his Senior Advisor on the Media, veteran journalist John Nagenda, as chief coordinator between the government and the filmmakers (Macdonald apparently offered him the role of chief torturer, which he refused).[4] Museveni also waived some taxes, notably VAT, for the filmmakers.[5] Others welcomed the commercial opportunities; an advertising executive named Paul Busharizi wrote, 'You might click your tongue at the perpetuation of the African stereotype of psychotic but disarmingly charming brutes, hopelessly gullible African masses and their obsequiousness towards foreigners, but for now all publicity, any publicity is good. Awareness is what *The Last King of Scotland* has provided for Brand Uganda.'[6] At the film's premiere in Uganda, President Museveni said it was the first time he had been to the cinema since 1959. He commented, 'I did not need any fiction. There was enough drama in real life.'[7] The most prominent Ugandan actor in the film was Abbey Mukiibi, who played Amin's security chief, Masanga. At the Ugandan premiere he was thrown off the red carpet and sent to the back of the queue to go through security checks. He seems to have borne no grudges about this treatment.[8]

President Museveni would, however, have found much fiction in *The Last King of Scotland*. In fact, the film is not even true to the novel it is based on. In the novel the 'hero', the Scottish doctor Nicholas Garrigan, is largely a passive bystander, a mere observer of the increasingly bizarre events in Amin's Uganda. In the film, however, he is an active participant in Amin's court. The plot of *The Last King of Scotland* follows the familiar story of Joseph Conrad's *Heart of Darkness* – an innocent (even ignorant) white European gets embroiled in an inexplicably violent African society, and becomes corrupted by its inherent evil. The story (notwithstanding Whitaker's scene-stealing presence) revolves around Garrigan. The Scottish doctor encounters Amin in the early days of his rule (1971). The new President takes an instant shine to him, makes him his personal physician, and lures him into the murderous politics of the presidential court. Real historical events are collapsed; the expulsion of Uganda's Asians (1972) is almost immediately followed by the hijacking of an Israeli airliner (1976). Garrigan

Myth and Reality in The Last King of Scotland

(rather unbelievably, not to say suicidally) seduces one of Amin's wives. Amin has her killed and Garrigan is tortured, before escaping, thanks to a Ugandan doctor, in the wake of the hijack.

In a talk at the Charleston Literary Festival in 2007, the book's author, Giles Foden, and the film's director, Kevin Macdonald, explained that a passive narrator does not work as the main character in a film and for that reason they rewrote the Garrigan character. And yet, whether passive or active, no such figure existed in real life. Amin certainly had British henchmen, most notoriously a middle-aged English ex-soldier named Bob Astles, but he was a very different, and considerably less attractive, character than the young Scottish doctor portrayed by James McAvoy.[9] Despite Whitaker's tremendous performance, placing a white character at the centre of the narrative tends to reduce the film to the standard sub-Conradian cliché of Africa as a blank contrast to European heroism (see Leopold 2009a; see Introduction, Eltringham and Hoffman, this volume).

In addition to the lack of an historical figure analogous to Nicholas Garrigan, most of the events depicted in the film did not actually take place. There are different versions of what really happened to Amin's wife, Kay, some of which echo the plot of the film (minus, of course, the fictional Garrigan). One of the more convincing is given by his British former Commanding Officer in the Kings African Rifles, who knew Amin well for a long time, Major Iain Grahame (1980: 160):

> [T]wo independent accounts of Kay's death, given to me at a later date, tally in all the essential details. Kay had a reputation for sleeping around and in the spring of 1974 had formed a relationship with a Muganda doctor called Mbalu-Mukasa ... although he was not a trained gynaecologist, Mbalu-Mukasa had performed a number of illegal abortions. The autopsy ... revealed that she had died from loss of blood, following an attempted surgical abortion. On 14 August, just before Kay's body was found in the boot of the doctor's car, the doctor himself was admitted to hospital, suffering from an overdose of sleeping pills. That same day he died ... What my two informants both told me was that Mbalu-Mukasa ... intentionally allowed her to die during the operation ... [He] I was told, carved up the body with the help of an assistant, hoping to dispose of it the following day. When he realized that his assistant had been arrested and confessed, he took his own life.

In addition to creating events, in letters to Ugandan newspapers, several Ugandans proudly pointed out cultural mistakes in the film (for example, an Acholi war dance performed with Bugandan tribal drums – these being two very different Ugandan tribes).[10] Even Forest Whitaker apparently worked up his part by eating nothing but the southern Ugandan staple food *matoke* (green bananas),[11] whereas the staple food for people from Amin's home area is made from millet. But, there is a qualitative difference between these unintentional errors and intentional distortions (see Introduction and Eltringham, this volume). A more serious distortion arises from Macdonald's decision to associate 1970s Uganda with a swinging social scene more appropriate to contemporary Europe, as witnessed in some of the wild parties depicted. On the DVD the director comments:

> I wanted to present an image of Africa in the early seventies that was very upbeat, very optimistic ... Uganda was particularly prosperous ... So we wanted to present an image of Africa that I think was very different from what people have. So we see the city, Kampala, feels like a very sexy, cool place.

In fact, Amin was, perhaps surprisingly, rather a prude in many matters. In 1972 he both banned women from wearing miniskirts, and refused entrance to Uganda to European men with longish hair. Garrigan's floppy locks in the film would certainly have been forbidden, as would the dress of the swinging dolly birds (to use the offensive contemporary language) in its party scenes.[12]

In a sense, however, this pedantry is to miss the point. Maybe this is not primarily a film about Ugandan history at all, but a film about Western ideas, or myths, about Africa. As such it is perhaps more true, more of a documentary, than it seems on the surface. A more profitable way of approaching the film, therefore, is to concentrate on its relationship with broader Ugandan society and social memory, a relation defined by a universal complicity between legend and reality related, of course, to a wider set of 'Western' ideas about Uganda, and Africa more generally (see Introduction, this volume). This relationship is recognized by Macdonald himself, in his DVD commentary on the film:

Myth and Reality in The Last King of Scotland

[R]eality and fantasy and history and fiction are all mixed up in Uganda around Amin, he's a sort of mythical figure, there's just so many tales about him, you never quite know what's true and not true. People can believe almost anything of him. And all the time we were there, we felt that we were sort of surrounded by his presence all the time. I had a dream that he was actually sitting on the end of my bed on the first night of shooting, which really freaked me out.

In a context in which the truth of a historical character is, therefore, so hard to pin down, *The Last King of Scotland* becomes an exercise in recognizing that truth and myth are difficult to disassociate.

As regards reality and history, Foden's original fictional novel acknowledges as a source the French filmmaker Barbet Schroeder's extraordinary 1974 documentary *General Idi Amin Dada (A Self Portrait)*.[13] Barbet's documentary gives a very intimate close-up of Amin at the height of his reign. It was made with Amin's full cooperation, and shows him at work and play. Macdonald has also acknowledged the influence of this documentary on the film and it was clearly a major inspiration both for various scenes in the film and for Forrest Whitaker's powerful, accurate and Oscar-winning portrayal of the dictator (as Macdonald's commentary on the DVD of the film concedes). But the facticity of the documentary as a source for the novel sits uneasily alongside other popular books on Amin that Foden acknowledges (such as Avirgan and Honey 1982, Grahame 1980, Hills 1975, Kyemba 1977, Listowel 1973, Martin 1974, Mazrui 1975, 1977 and Smith 1980). Perhaps the greatest literary influence on the original novel of *The Last King of Scotland*, however, was the 1977 book by Henry Kyemba (once Amin's Minister of Health) entitled *State of Blood*. This memoir, which has been in print ever since, contains many if not most of the events, or stories, that have since become irretrievably attached to Amin's name; tales of cannibalism, fridges full of body parts, and the like.

I have written elsewhere about the popular journalistic books and memoirs about Amin and his rule (see Leopold 2009a), as well as about the history of the region and the ethnic background from which Amin came (see, e.g. Leopold 2005, 2006, 2009b). Here I

27

briefly want to make it clear that the images of savagery, violence and cannibalism characteristic of most published accounts of Amin's life were in fact associated, long before his birth, with his home region (West Nile district, in the north-west of Uganda, by the borders with Sudan and the Congo) and with the complex ethnic background from which he came. These stories were propagated both by British and other European writers, and by Ugandans from the south of the country. The more extreme versions of the cannibalism myth, for example, emanated not from the international media but from southern Ugandan sources such as Henry Kyemba. There is, moreover, some evidence that Amin may have propagated, or at least not discouraged, such stories, as a means of instilling additional terror in potential opponents (Leopold 2005: 58–61). British colonialists saw the men of West Nile as natural warriors, 'the best material for soldiery in Africa' as Lord Lugard put it (Moyse-Bartlett 1956: 50). Lugard used them as the core of the colonial troops, the King's African Rifles (KAR), who carved out and preserved Britain's East African empire. Amin himself grew up within the world of the KAR and so, whatever he became, the British army played a large part in making him it.[14] (There is no space in this chapter to justify these statements, but ample evidence will be found in my published work cited throughout this chapter.) However, despite my criticisms of the popular image of Amin, I have no interest in joining the increasing volume of revisionist accounts of his rule being published in Uganda today.[15]

That stories of cannibalism, as told by Kyemba and others, would resurface in *The Last King of Scotland* certainly worried Amin's family, who objected to the film. Amin's son, Taban Amin (who, under President Museveni, became a very senior officer in Uganda's External Security Organization), threatened to sue the producers of the film, telling the government newspaper, 'They are going to act that he ate people. I stayed with him for so long but I never saw any human flesh'.[16] In his recent book *Idi Amin: Hero or Villain?* (2010), Jaffar Amin, his third son, is asked by his co-writer, Margaret Akulia, 'Are there any "threads of truth" in any of the story lines in the hit movie?', to which he replies, 'Pure Hollywood. Completely off the wall, hook, line and sinker – entertainment par excellence ... This storyline is not even in the fictitious novel' (Amin and Akulia 2010: 528).[17] In fact, Macdonald took a sceptical attitude to such claims. In his commentary on the DVD version of the film, he perceptively states that:

> The international press were saying, 'He's a cannibal, he eats peoples' livers'. There's not really any evidence for that, but it's one thing that's often said about him even now. We asked around a lot, we talked to people who were very close to Amin and his government, etc., but nobody had any first-hand evidence. I suspect it probably wasn't true. It was just something that the press built up around him to make him seem even more savage, more 'other'. I often thought when making the movie that in a way if Amin hadn't existed the Western press would have had to invent him. It was just the perfect story ... hilarious, bizarre but also murderous, terrifying.

In other words, while Macdonald recognized that his film was fictitious (based on a self-consciously fictitious novel), when it came to cannibalism he chose to privilege fact. While the mythical figure of Amin (with its contradictory elements of attraction, repulsion and buffoonery) is replicated in the film, a key element of that myth (cannibalism) is omitted.

The King in Waiting

One aspect of *The Last King of Scotland* which does have more than a grain of truth is Amin's interest in Scotland (or at least in its potential for annoying the English). On his only visit to Britain in July 1971, a few months after seizing power, he insisted on visiting Scotland (after meeting the Queen in London) and announced his intention of swimming in the sea there. In the event, he contented himself with an afternoon's shopping in Edinburgh (he wanted to create a pipe band in the Ugandan army, and bought a number of kilts for the soldiers), after an exhausting programme of formal dinners, cocktail parties, military parades and visiting monuments. In 1973, in an interview with the BBC journalist Tom Mangold, he was asked why he insisted on Scottish rather than English regiments training his troops (Mangold suggesting that this was a racist preference). Amin rose to the bait:

> I haven't many English soldiers. You should know that even during the war most of the time I have been with the Scottish and within my blood I love them very much and like them very much and I feel very happy when I am with them because you find that in England the English themselves they are the racialists completely, not the Scottish. If you go to Scotland you will talk to the people. They will welcome you in their house. If you go to the hotel they will sit with you and you will eat together. If you go to England where there is English they do not want to sit near you. If they see a black man they say he is a monkey or a dog. They would rather sit with a dog than with a black man. The English are racialistic. In England, especially in London, a black man in a hotel, you cannot find him sitting with the English. Like you have something smelling in your body. You can notice this in London, but not in Scotland; I like them very much because they are very good people.[18]

In late 1974 Amin was apparently approached by a group of extreme Scottish nationalists, calling themselves the Provisional Government of Scotland, who asked for his help in putting their case to the UN and other international bodies. On 30 December Amin sent a very lengthy telegram to, amongst others, the British Prime Minister, the Secretary Generals of the UN and the Organization of African Unity, the Soviet leader Leonid Brezhnev, Chairman Mao Tse Tung, Queen Elizabeth II, President Giscard d'Estaing of France, Palestinian leader Yasser Arafat, and Libya's Colonel Gaddafi. Amin writes that:

> [T]he people of Scotland are tired of being exploited by the English. For a long time, England has thrived on the energies and brains of the Scottish people. Yet the wealth they have derived from Scotland has not been ploughed back. Instead, they have built multiple industries in England in order to provide employment for the English people leaving the people of Scotland in economic slavery ... They are now working out plans to exploit Scotland further by grabbing the money which is to be obtained from the North Sea oil ... [that is] part of Scotland's natural resources which must be exploited for the good of the Scottish people ... The leaders of the Scottish Provisional Government have also asked me to inform you that they are fed up with English discrimination both within England itself and also in countries like South Africa and Rhodesia. The

people of Scotland are absolutely social people and hate colour bar of any sort. They are therefore completely embarrassed by what goes on in England, Rhodesia and South Africa, and the daily massacres being carried out by the English in Northern Ireland. They have also informed me that the English are the ones highly involved in the support of Zionist Israelis against the Palestinians.[19] On the other hand, the Scottish leaders have informed me that they want to be friendly with all the people of the world and that they would like to be completely detached from the English. Unless they are given independence peacefully they will take up arms and fight the English until they regain their freedom.

The telegram includes a lengthy account of Scottish history, apparently taken from some booklets given to Amin by the 'Provisional Government'. It goes on to state:

> The leaders of the Scottish Provisional Government assured me that they consider me, General Amin, as their leader and they have made me Chairman of the Uganda/Scottish community. They pledged that no Scottish man or woman, young or old, will be against me, even though there may be a few Ugandans who after being brainwashed and confused by the English, may be against me.[20]

The British government responded by refusing to acknowledge Amin's 1974 Christmas card to the Prime Minister. The Foreign Office stated: 'This would seem particularly inappropriate in the wake of Amin's presentation of the case of a "provisional Scottish Government" to the UN and other international bodies and leaders.'[21]

The only contemporary evidence I have found for Amin actually calling himself the King of Scotland, however, is in the published diaries of Sir Peter Allen, a (very English) High Court Judge in Amin's Uganda, who apparently wrote on 22 June 1975, 'On several occasions Amin has even boasted that he has been invited to become King of Scotland' (Allen 2000: 404, published after the novel, though before the film). But the episode of the Provisional Scottish Government does demonstrate a major aspect of the portrayal of Amin in virtually every first-hand account of him and echoed in *The Last King of Scotland*, both film and book: his almost self-parodying sense of humour, usually characterized by the word 'buffoon'. This is exemplified by his many eccentric messages to world leaders; such as his offer to marry the British Queen, as well as his establishment of a fund to aid Britain in its economic crisis of the mid 1970s, in which he sent a lorry load of bananas for 'the starving British people'. It is an aspect of Amin's personality which is deeply embarrassing to many contemporary Ugandans.[22] I suspect he learned how to play the fool, and to play up to racial stereotypes, to please his British superior officers in the army, but perhaps he also simply had a particular sense of humour. In the film Amin's sense of humour seems to be one of the things which attract the young Scottish doctor Garrigan to the dictator in the first place, and it was certainly an aspect of his personality which interested the French documentary director Barbet Schroeder. In an interview for the DVD version of his documentary, Schroeder says that Amin 'is somebody extremely charming, very funny. There is something in him that is totally disarming and a life force, and an innocence that is extraordinary. At the same time, you know that this is a face of evil'.

Amin 'The Hero'

The Scottish Provisional Government telegram also demonstrates Amin's anti-colonialist attitudes, which tend to be more favourably received in contemporary Uganda than his buffoonery. In a series of articles in the independent Ugandan newspaper *The Monitor* in 2007, for example, the journalist Timothy Kalyegira argued that Amin was a patriot who was the most effective of Uganda's leaders and has been slandered by the West. Similarly, on 10 October 2007 Kalyegira wrote that:

> Amin ... struggled to maintain Uganda's stance against Western 'imperialism', what that brought for Amin when he turned onto British and Israeli economic and military interests in Uganda, was a sudden hostile media campaign from the Western world that left him with a world-infamous reputation as the murderer of 500,000 Ugandans, a claim that these days is proving increasingly and embarrassingly impossible to maintain.

This attitude, and its delicate relationship with rehabilitating Amin was also apparent in a 2005 interview given by Forest Whitaker with the *New Vision* newspaper:

> I'm not trying to defend Amin ... the Amin I found was not a good man, but not the monster as presented ... When I first decided to act Amin, I had that perception of Amin as presented by the west ... After I started [researching] his rule and life, what was being portrayed in the west was not his real image ... Now, I have come to appreciate and understand why he made certain decisions at certain times. He did things like other big men who did things that helped their countries.

Whittaker went on to note that, in particular, he appreciated Amin's virulent abhorrence of European colonialism.[23]

John Nagenda, however, writing in *Prospect* magazine two years later was clearly troubled by Whitaker's approach:

> Forest Whitaker ... gets into the mass-murderer-cum-genial giant in a way that almost frightens. I had asked him ... whether he would play Amin as a raging tyrant, destroying everything in sight. He looked surprised. 'Of course, Amin is a hero', he whispered ... I squared my shoulders. It was true, I said, that when Amin first took over power in Uganda, he was feted by many. And that he had an undeniable geniality which, with his largeness of body, and his infectious love of life (would that he had spared more of it) was attractive to many. Also, for a man of hardly any education, the way he picked things up, including the English language, was staggering. What might he have been with more advantages at birth, such as education and family affection? But when ruling started being difficult, it was as if hot devils exploded within him. The killing started and quickly shot out of control. This man was the opposite of a hero. Whether Forest listened to any of this and was diverted from his first reading, I know not. The answer is plain in the Amin he brought to the screen, a frightening monster, but a child of God.[24]

Nagenda himself did not meet Amin during the latter's presidency, having spent most of the 1970s in the United States (J. Nagenda, pers. comm.).

When the film came out, most Ugandan commentators, while recognizing many of the film's scenes as fiction, were impressed by the wider accuracy of Whitaker's portrayal of Amin, not simply as a monster, but as a charming, humorous, clever and charismatic monster. Professor Ali Mazrui, who certainly knew Amin, summed up this view in an interview with the independent Ugandan newspaper *The Sunday Monitor*:

> My ex-wife and I compared notes on *The Last King of Scotland*. We thought it was a relatively good portrayal of Idi Amin, independently of each other, and did not regard it as a distortion. Your idea that people love him or hate him is correct and that he was a mixture of many things is also correct. That he laughed a lot and could be extremely cruel is also correct. None of these is impossible in a single person and many of them were there.[25]

In this way, the film (especially Whitaker's performance) appears to have captured the core of Amin's mythical status: his ability to attract and repel in equal measure.

As mentioned, the most important factual source for the film was certainly Barbet Schroeder's 1974 documentary film, *General Idi Amin Dada (A Self-Portrait)*. Not only did this powerful film form the basis of Whitaker's vividly successful impersonation of the man himself, but entire scenes from *The Last King of Scotland* were, as Macdonald acknowledges, copied frame for frame from the original documentary (for example, Amin's swimming race with his Cabinet). However, Schroeder himself took his lead from the classic directors of the French post-war New Wave movement especially the anthropological filmmaker, Jean Rouche who, like Schroeder, sought to deconstruct the distinction between fact and fiction, documentary and story. In his interview on the DVD version of the *A Self Portrait*, Schroeder remarks: 'I can't conceive of making a fiction film without making a full research about everything concerning that movie ... So I do a documentary work on every fiction film and I try to introduce fiction into the documentaries that I make.' It is easy to see why this attitude of Schroeder's would have attracted him to the ambiguous character of Amin, whose personality and reputation constantly demonstrated the interconnections between fact, fiction and myth. His factual portrayal of Amin is perhaps so close to Whitaker's fictional one because of his awareness of what one might term the power of myth within the myth of power. As Schroeder puts it, '[Amin] has such a strong screen presence. This is of course a caricature, it's also a caricature even of a dictator. But it has something very true. I think that every political man is portrayed in Amin Dada.'

Conclusion

Truth is truth, fiction is fiction, and both the novel and film of *The Last King of Scotland* are unashamedly fiction. Nevertheless, as I have also shown, in the forward to the novel Foden cites a number of sources which at least purport to be fact, while the film itself leans heavily on Schroeder's documentary. But, I would suggest that both the book and film are, above all, meditations on the power of myth, where myth is neither truth nor fiction. It operates in the realm of metaphor. It may be *literally* false, but *metaphorically* true – indeed sometimes, in a sense, myths or legends may be truer to the realities of life than a pure recitation of fully confirmed facts (see Introduction, this volume). The reception of Whitaker's portrayal of Amin, among Ugandans and others who knew the dictator, demonstrates that a great performance may operate as a truth over and above any factual inaccuracies of the storyline. Going further, the events recounted in the popular books on Amin and echoed in the novel and film, may or may not be literally true, but either way they represent a (perhaps metaphorical) reality that those who lived through his rule experienced. The cannibalism myth, for example, clearly resonates with the widespread African use of metaphors of eating to understand both corruption in the narrow sense and illegitimate political power in a wider sense (see Bayart 1993), and suggest that in local terms the metaphor represents a wider reality. Another aspect of the legend which deserves to be printed is recounted by Barbet Schroeder in his interview on the DVD of *A Self Portrait*. After Amin's fall from power, he restored the couple of minutes he had been forced to cut from his documentary, with one exception, a key lack: 'One line of voice-over got lost. It was the last sentence of the film ... [over the image of Amin giving a speech, the commentary went] "After a century of colonization let

35

us not forget that it is partially a deformed image of ourselves that Idi Amin Dada reflects back at us'". The uncomfortable self-recognition that viewers experience in watching Forest Whitaker and the simultaneous attraction and repulsion we feel resonates with the ambiguous place that Amin holds in global imageries of Africa.

Notes

1. Coincidentally, the year Uganda attained independence.
2. Macdonald directed the documentary *One Day in September* (1999) concerned with the murder of Israeli athletes at the 1972 Munich Olympics.
3. K. Kabuye in the Ugandan Government-owned newspaper the *New Vision*, 9 June 2005.
4. J. Nagenda in the Ugandan Government-owned newspaper the *New Vision*, 15 September 2006.
5. J. Nagenda in the Ugandan Government-owned newspaper the *New Vision*, 30 June 2006.
6. Quoted in *New Vision*, 4 March 2007.
7. President Y.K. Museveni in *New Vision*, 18 February 2007.
8. *New Vision*, 22 February 2007.
9. Considerably older than the fictional Garrigan, and English rather than Scottish, Astles worked for the Ugandan civil service and declared himself to be a Ugandan. Unlike Garrigan in the film, he was an associate of Amin long before he became President. He is said to have worked for both the Ugandan and British secret services in the 1960s, under Amin's predecessor, Milton Obote. When Amin was head of Obote's army, he and Astles were both involved in a secret operation, supported by Israel, to supply gold stolen from the Congo to rebels in southern Sudan (see, e.g., U.K. National Archives, file FCO 31/493, 1969).
10. See the Ugandan Government-owned newspaper the *New Vision*, 17 April 2007.
11. According to MacDonald's commentary included on the DVD version of *The Last King of Scotland*.
12. See documents in the U.K. National Archives, file FCO 31/1324, 'Political Developments in Uganda 1972'.
13. Schroeder's subtitle is justified not least because Amin himself had the 'final cut' of the documentary, threatening to harm 150 French citizens in Uganda unless certain cuts were made (amounting to two minutes and twenty-one seconds of the original film). A digital version, cuts restored (and including much new material) was released on DVD in 2002.
14. Of course, many Africans went through the KAR without becoming anything like Amin.

15. Several Ugandan writers have recently compared Amin favourably with Uganda's current leadership, and have written positive accounts of his rule (see Sembuya 2009; Amin and Akulia 2010).
16. Taban Amin, quoted in *New Vision*, 20 August 2005.
17. Jaffar is, however, complimentary about Whitaker's performance.
18. Transcribed in the U.K. National Archives, file FCO 31/1586, 'President Idi Amin of Uganda 1973'.
19. It should perhaps be noted here that the coup which put Amin into power was itself actively supported and aided by the Israelis, though he later fell out with them.
20. The telegram can be found in the U.K. National Archives, file FCO 31/1785, 'Political Relations Uganda/U.K. December 1974'.
21. Letter from J.D.F. Holt (Foreign and Commonwealth Office) to Patrick Wright, Private Secretary to the Prime Minister, 10 Downing Street, dated 2 January 1975. This can be found in the UK National Archives, file FCO 31/1954, 'Political Relations Uganda/U.K. January–February 1975'.
22. See, for example, various comments in the letters columns of the *New Vision*, 1 February 2007 and 9 February 2007.
23. Forest Whitaker, quoted in *New Vision*, 13 August 2005.
24. J. Nagenda, quoted in *Prospect* magazine (U.K.), 17 January 2007.
25. Quoted in the independent Ugandan newspaper, the *Sunday Monitor*, 16 August 2009.

Filmography

Ford, J. (Dir.) 1962. *The Man Who Shot Liberty Valance* (Paramount Pictures, John Ford Productions).
Macdonald, K. (Dir.) 1999. *One Day in September* (Passion Pictures, Arthur Cohn Productions, British Broadcasting Corporation (BBC), British Screen Productions, Dan Valley Film AG, European Co-production Fund, Soros Documentary Fund of the Open Society Movement).
Macdonald, K. (Dir.) 2006. *The Last King of Scotland* (Fox Searchlight Pictures, DNA Films, FilmFour, U.K. Film Council, Scottish Screen, Cowboy Films, Slate Films, Tatfilm).
Schroeder, B. (Dir.) 1974. *General Idi Amin Dada (A Self Portrait)* (Figaro Films, Mara Films, Television Recontre).

References

Allen, P. 2000. *Interesting Times; Ugandan Diaries 1955–1986*. Lewes: The Book Guild Ltd.

Amin, J. and M. Akulia. 2010. *Idi Amin: Hero or Villain?: His Son Jaffar Amin and Other People Speak*. Vancouver: Millennium Global Publishers.
Avirgan, T. and M. Honey. 1982. *War in Uganda: The Legacy of Idi Amin*. London: Zed Press.
Bayart, J.F. 1993. *The State in Africa: The Politics of the Belly*. London: Longman.
Grahame, I. 1980. *Amin and Uganda: A Personal Memoir*. London: Granada Publishing.
Hills, D. 1975. *The White Pumpkin*. London: George Allen and Unwin.
Kimborough, R. (ed.). 1988. *Heart of Darkness. Joseph Conrad Norton Critical Edition*, 8th ed. New York and London: W.W. Norton and Co.
Kyemba, H. 1977. *State of Blood: The Inside Story of Idi Amin*. London: Corgi Books.
Leopold, M. 1999. '"The War in the North": Ethnicity in Ugandan Press Explanations of Conflict, 1996–97', in T. Allen and J. Seaton (eds), *The Media of Conflict: War Reporting and Representations of Ethnic Violence*. London: Zed Press, pp. 219–43.
Leopold, M. 2005. *Inside West Nile: Violence, History and Representation on an African Frontier*. Oxford: James Currey; Santa Fe: School of American Research Press; Kampala: Fountain Publishers.
Leopold, M. 2006. 'The Story of the "One-Elevens": Legacies of Slavery in North West Uganda', *Africa: Journal of the International African Institute* 76(2): 180–99.
Leopold, M. 2009a. 'Sex, Violence and History in the Lives of Idi Amin: Postcolonial Masculinity as Masquerade', *Journal of Postcolonial Writing* 45(3): 321–30.
Leopold, M. 2009b. 'Crossing the Line; 100 Years of the North-West Uganda/South Sudan Border', *Journal of East African Studies* 3(3): 464–78.
Listowel, J. 1973. *Amin*. Dublin and London: IUP Books.
Martin, D. 1974. *General Amin*. London: Faber and Faber.
Mazrui, A.A. 1975. *Soldiers and Kinsmen in Uganda: The Making of a Military Ethnography*. Beverley Hills and London: Sage Publications.
Mazrui, A.A. (ed.). 1977. *The Warrior Tradition in Modern Africa*. Leiden: E.J. Brill.
Moyse-Bartlett, H. 1956. *The Kings African Rifles: A Study in the Military History of East and Central Africa, 1890–1945*. Aldershot: Gale and Polden Ltd.
Sembuya, C. 2009. *The Other Side of Idi Amin Dada*. Kampala: Sest Holdings.
Smith, G.I. 1980. *Ghosts of Kampala*. London: Weidenfeld and Nicholson.

Two

Black Hawk Down
Recasting U.S. Military History at Somali Expense

Lidwien Kapteijns

The Hollywood film *Black Hawk Down* revisits the history of the U.S. military Operation Irene in Mogadishu, Somalia on 3 October 1993.[1] The battle that ensued consisted of sixteen hours of intense urban warfare, during which Somali fighters downed three Black Hawk combat helicopters, killed nineteen U.S. soldiers, and dragged some of their bodies through the streets of Mogadishu. The film was based on the 1999 book of the same title by Mark Bowden and a film script by Ken Nolan. It was shot in Morocco, directed by Ridley Scott and produced by Jerry Bruckheimer, both veterans of the genre of the war film. Made in close collaboration with the U.S. military (Department of Defence) and released in December 2001, it injected its portrayal of an apparent U.S. military defeat in Somalia in 1993 (shortly after the end of the Cold War) into a moment at which the U.S. military had just sent its troops into Afghanistan, shortly after 11 September 2001. *Black Hawk Down* is therefore deeply embedded in the domestic and international politics and policy struggles of both periods (see Lawrence and McGarrahan 2008: 448).

Black Hawk Down has given rise to a small body of analytically superb scholarship, whose only drawback is its limited knowledge base and understanding of Somalia history. Here, I will draw on the strengths of this scholarship,[2] but focus on how *Black Hawk Down* represents the situation in Somalia in 1993 and portrays Somalis as political and military actors.

Like other blockbuster films produced by the globally networked entertainment industry called Hollywood,[3] *Black Hawk Down* is a political technology – to use Mark Lacy's (2003: 624) term – that has the power and reach to influence the views and values of millions of viewers. A study of the strategies of persuasion pursued by its makers can shed light on the 'preferred' political readings the film enables.[4] Here, I will first examine how the filmmakers' claims to accuracy and immediacy (that the film gives viewers an immediate/unmediated experience of what *actually* happened) and their rationale for close collaboration with the U.S. military mutually constitute each other and shape the content of the film and the 'truths' it puts forward. This and other strategies, three of which I consider in detail, produce (and are designed to produce) very specific political messages. First, through its framing of the events of October 1993, *Black Hawk Down* conceals and misrepresents U.S. involvement in Somalia prior to 1993, which contributed to state collapse and violence there. Second, through the 'mythic enhancement' of the characters representing the U.S. military and 'mythic diminishment' of those portraying Somalis,[5] the film misrepresents both, I will argue, to the glory of the former and at the expense of the latter. By enabling viewers' 'moral proximity' to the U.S. military and moral distance from the Somalis, the latter are reduced to providing a depraved and savage foil to the innocence and nobility (even if also the human imperfection) of the latter.[6] Finally, through the strategy of 'mythic condensation'[7] in how the film provides closure to the narrative and recasts the U.S. players portrayed in it, the film not only comes to constitute a tribute to, and glorification of the U.S. military but also – at the transformative post 9/11 moment of its release – enables a reading that affirms the necessity of U.S. military intervention in the world. All this is achieved on the backs of the Somalis, who remain woefully under- and misrepresented.

Summary of the Film and Historical Background to Somalia in 1993

Black Hawk Down's opening scene shows how a Somali gunman takes possession of a truckload of Red Cross food aid by opening fire on unarmed Somali civilians. Two men of the U.S. Task Force Ranger (TFR), who observe this from the air, ask permission to intervene but are told that UN rules of engagement do not allow this. Having established TFR's just cause, the film then quickly moves to its main subject, the military operation of 3 October 1993 (Operation Irene), in which Somali fighters brought down three Black Hawk combat helicopters, killed nineteen U.S. soldiers and dragged the corpses of several of them through the city streets. The film moves back and forth between the different groups of participants as they experience this sixteen-hour gun battle. On the American side, it shows the men of TFR as they relax and chat in their barracks before the action; as they rope down into the city from Black Hawk helicopters; and as they get pinned down and start dying. It interweaves this storyline with three others: that of the un-armoured truck convoy that gets hopelessly lost and suffers heavy casualties; that of the U.S. helicopter pilots who circle high above this hell but fail to give good directions; and that of General Garrison of the Joint Operations Centre who observes the action far away on a screen. The Somali side receives much less attention. The film portrays only four named Somali individuals; most others form faceless and fanatical mobs whose relentless attacks on the stranded U.S. soldiers continue in spite of the tons of lead the U.S. combat helicopters discharge at them from the night sky. The film chronicles Operation Irene until the last survivors, rescued by a convoy of Pakistani and Malaysian UN trucks, reach safety in the early morning of 4 October. Because the filmmakers set out to portray modern, high-tech, urban warfare and the bodily and emotional experiences of U.S. soldiers in the heat

41

of battle as realistically as possible, the film consists largely of deafening and intensely graphic battle scenes with limited narrative. The minimal context it provides to this episode of the UN/U.S. military humanitarian intervention in Somalia between 1992 and 1995 takes the form of short texts (or legends) at the beginning and end of the film.

The Somali Republic came into existence in 1960, when two former colonies, Italian Somaliland and the British Somaliland Protectorate, gained political independence and formed a political union. The era of civilian administrations that followed (1960–1991) was characterized by a flourishing of political and cultural nationalism, which expressed itself, among other things, in an active (but unsuccessful) commitment to bringing neighbouring Somali regions into the new nation state. In October 1969 a coup d'état led by Mohamed Siyad Barre ushered in the era of military rule (1969–1991). Although Barre's regime was autocratic and violent from the very beginning, its purposeful investment in nationalist cultural production and emphasis on self-help and 'scientific socialist' development made it initially quite popular. However, especially after Somalia's defeat in the war with Ethiopia (1977–1978), the regime's increasingly violent political repression and divide-and-rule policies, its economic corruption and the purposeful undermining of public institutions led to the emergence of armed opposition fronts. In its attempts to defeat these the regime used large-scale violence against the civilians it (solely on the basis of their clan backgrounds) associated with these armed opposition groups. In January 1991, as the regime collapsed, some of these fronts' leaders, in the hope of monopolizing state power themselves, turned to terror warfare against civilians it constructed as 'enemy clans'. The clan-cleansing campaign and widespread militia warfare that followed caused the massive famine that in December 1992 triggered the UN/U.S. intervention of which the *Black Hawk Down* episode was a part. At the time of writing Somali civil war violence, although transformed, is ongoing.[8]

Truth Claims and Collaboration with the U.S. Military

Although partnership between Hollywood and the U.S. military and in the production of war films is nothing new, in the making of *Black Hawk Down* the scale and range of this collaboration exceeded earlier instances. As Bruckheimer himself put it, 'Even though we have a great relationship with the government, this was a much bigger operation than anything we had attempted before, even on *Top Gun* and *Pearl Harbor*. We were talking about actual troop deployment' (Nolan 2002: 163). He was not speaking metaphorically. In order to re-enact the 'insertion' of the men of the U.S. Task Force Ranger (TFR) into Mogadishu, Bruckheimer and Scott persuaded the U.S. and Moroccan governments to allow into Morocco four Black Hawk and four Little Bird combat helicopters, together with the pilots and crew to operate them, including 100 men of the same Rangers regiment that had participated in the incident in Mogadishu in October 1993 (Lawrence and McGarrahan 2008: 172). Obtaining this kind of military hardware and specialized military personnel for the film – provided by the U.S. military under the guise of a formal training mission at the low cost of $2.2 million (Lisle and Pepper 2005: 172) – was the first and most significant aspect of the U.S. military's involvement with the film. It became a central element of the filmmakers' claim of telling the story authentically and accurately, which also fulfilled the condition the U.S. military had set for its input (Lisle and Pepper 2005: 174).

The second aspect of this involvement was the presence on site in Morocco of three military advisers and coaches whose job it was to 'keep it real'. These were a Vietnam veteran and former Navy SEAL and two veterans of Operation Irene itself (Nolan 2002: 162, 170). Director Ridley Scott has described how these two sat beside him throughout the shoot, quibbling with him about how to represent the military accurately (Gross 2005: 210–11).

Third, the film's actors received a week-long orientation and training at the three U.S. military forts where the U.S. soldiers they represented had been based: Fort Benning, Georgia (for the

Rangers), Fort Bragg, North Carolina (for the men of Delta Force), and Fort Campbell, Kentucky (for the helicopter pilots called the Night Stalkers) (*BHD* 2003 2b; also Nolan 2002: 164–65). Here the actors not only learned how to hold a gun, blow open doors and traverse a city street as if under fire, but also, by the filmmakers' design, to gain respect for the military and for the soldiers they were to portray. As the actors' reflections about this experience demonstrate, this goal was fully met (see Nolan 2002: 163; *BHD* 2003 2b).

During the shoot in Morocco, this respect deepened further. The film script describes it as follows: 'The Military and movie makers began to form something of a mutual admiration society – cast and crew members in absolute awe of the commitment and precision of the Rangers and SOAR pilots and vice-versa' (Nolan 2002: 174). The filmmakers so much identified with the military aspect of the film that the documentary about how the film was made couches the different aspects of the film's production in military terms: the documentary as a whole is called *The Essence of Combat: Making Black Hawk Down*. The section about the shooting of the film in Morocco is titled 'Battlefield Morocco'; that about the sound track, 'Hymn for the fallen'; the episode about special digital effects, 'Digital warriors'; and the conclusion, which includes reflections on the wider meanings of the film by those who participated in making it, is called 'After action report' (*BHD* 2003 2e).

The mutual admiration between filmmakers and the U.S. military largely derived from succeeding in 'keeping it real'. In the book on which the film was based, Bowden's *Black Hawk Down*, the author had described his goal as producing a 'gripping and historically correct account' (Bowden 2000a: 333). Restating this later, Bowden used a visual metaphor that further emphasized his desire for immediacy: he had aspired to be 'a window pane' uncluttered by his own judgements and reflections, he wrote, so that his readers could experience the events as if they actually stood in the soldiers' shoes (*BHD* 2003 2a; see also Bowden 2000b). Scott expressed his commitment to accuracy and immediacy in similar terms, noting that he wanted to get 'as close to documentary credibility and accuracy as possible' (*BHD* 2003 2c. See Introduction and Hoffman, this volume, regarding the mimicry of documentary in fictional films). Elsewhere Scott stated, 'It's what I do ... putting the audience actually in the scene in the delivery and on the receiving end. Making them feel it' (Foden 2002).

It is obvious that the accuracy and immediacy to which the filmmakers aspired focused first and foremost on the technical accuracy of the re-enaction of the military operation, on the one hand, and the experience of the U.S. soldiers executing it, on the other. Emphasizing the former, Bowden wrote, 'What viewers see in the film is without question the most authentic depiction of modern soldiery ever filmed' (Bowden 2002: xi). Commenting on the latter (the experience of the soldiers), Scott claimed that his film presented 'the universal soldier's point of view' (Nolan 2002: 174). Both men connected their insights to the claim that accuracy and immediacy allowed the film to transcend politics (ibid.; Bowden 2002: xii).

Lisle and Pepper (2005: 181–82) have a different take on the results of the filmmakers' pursuit of accuracy and immediacy. They use Claudia Springer's (1988) notion of 'cinematic excess' or 'excess of spectacle' to argue that what differentiates *Black Hawk Down* from other films in the war film genre 'is the extent to which spectacle is in excess of the narrative' (2005: 182), especially in the scenes of the middle section, which 'contain almost no dialogue and are little more than spectacular cinematic amalgamations of gunfire, running soldiers, evocative music, swarming Somalis and crashing helicopters'. They argue that the lack of 'an anchoring narrative that orders and directs audience responses', leads to the dissipation of a unified political message and meaning. While I agree with Lisle and Pepper that excess of spectacle is part of the film's claims to truth and accuracy, as I will explain below, I see it as a strategy that enables and promotes (rather than dissipates) specific and highly political meanings and readings.

In what follows I will analyse how specific filmic strategies produce certain aspects of the 3 October episode as accurate and unmediated, while concealing, displacing, excluding, and misrepresenting others.

Framing the Narrative: Concealing UN/U.S. Contributions to the Violence in Somalia

The first filmic strategy to be examined is that of the narrative framing of the events of 3 October 1993 at the opening of the film. Scott decided to cut this framing to a bare minimum (see Hoffman, this volume, for a discussion of limited context in opening text). However, this act of filmic condensation, which reduces the background history to eleven brief sections of screen text, seriously misrepresents the situation in Somalia in 1993 both by what it makes explicit and what it omits.

The opening text introduces Somalia as a place where 'famine on a biblical scale', caused by 'years of warfare among rival clans' led to the deaths of 300,000 Somalis. We are told that the most powerful Somali warlord, Mohamed Farah Aidiid, seized international food aid by force and that, to prevent starvation, 20,000 U.S. marines delivered food and restored order. When Aidiid, in the wake of the marines' departure, slaughtered twenty-four Pakistani soldiers, and began targeting 'American personnel', a company of elite U.S. soldiers (those of Task Force Ranger), were sent in to remove him (ibid.).

A number of omissions are immediately obvious. The first one is that the film presents the U.S. military intervention in Somalia in December 1992 as simply humanitarian, ignoring the domestic and international agendas that underlay it. Analyzing the full context of this intervention lies beyond the scope of this essay.[9] However, given that the U.S. military is the film's central subject, its objectives are of relevance here. In 1992, at the end of the Cold War and on the eve of the presidency of the allegedly virulently anti-military Clinton, the U.S. military was deeply worried about its future role and budget. This was one major reason why President George Bush decided on a military intervention in Somalia in the last month of his presidency. George Bush and General Colin Powell, the Chairman of the Joint Chiefs of Staff, had other domestic reasons for intervening in Somalia as well. As Blumenthal argues in his 1993 article, the Somali intervention conformed to the doctrine Powell had developed in response to U.S. military failure in Vietnam, namely that 'only invincible force, achieving success in the shortest time possible, could justify the use of force at all' (1993: 54). To Blumenthal's mind 'the Mission was only incidentally about the Somalis: Somalia simply provided an arena for George Bush and Colin Powell to transform past failure into certain success' (1993: 51). However, it was not just 'past failure' that motivated U.S. leaders. After all, the Gulf War of early 1991, a war without large numbers of boots on the ground or U.S. casualties, had been a resounding military success. Repeating this success in Somalia, which was marginal to U.S. national interests and had no oil (at least as yet) was a golden opportunity to prove that President Bush's 'New World Order' was not just talk. A Christmastime humanitarian military intervention in Somalia, in which the U.S. could use the UN to experiment with assertive peace-making, could showcase the unselfish contributions the U.S. would make as sole superpower in the post-Cold War world. Military hubris and (on the part of the President) perhaps naïve humanitarianism and concern about his legacy were therefore also part of U.S. motives for intervention. In contrast, *Black Hawk Down* presents the U.S. military intervention in Somalia as only humanitarian.

A second omission is that the film conceals the fact that U.S. political and military involvement in Somalia did not begin with the famine in 1992 but goes back to the early 1980s, when the U.S., in the context of the Cold War, began to financially and militarily support military dictator Mohamed Siyad Barre, who increasingly used large-scale violence against civilians. This aid consisted both of military aid (estimated at $163.5 million between 1980 and 1988) and economic aid. The latter, which to a large extent consisted of USAID-disbursed commodity and cash grants that were particularly vulnerable to be stolen by government officials, was in the period 1982–1988 as high as $490 million, with overall donor support to

Somalia between 1980 and 1989 amounting to $2.5 billion (Rawson 1994: 164–69). This did not include aid brought in by UNHCR, which, together with the World Food Organization and the NGO called CARE, pumped millions of dollars into Somalia to feed refugees from the Somali–Ethiopian war of 1977–1978, whose numbers, though continuously inflated by the government, were estimated at 400,000 to one million (see also Brons 2001: 187; Maren 1997: 125–30). The collusion of these relief and aid organizations with the military regime's deceitful diversion of this refugee aid and the disastrous consequences for those who either tried to grow food in Somalia or grew dependent on hand-outs empowered the military dictator and his political clients while destroying the country and its people politically and economically (see Maren 1997).

Moreover, when this military regime collapsed in January 1991 and General Mohamed Farah Aidiid, in an attempt at monopolizing power, became the driving force of a campaign of clan cleansing that killed tens of thousands and expelled hundreds of thousands of Somali civilians, the U.S., fully preoccupied with fighting the Gulf War, did nothing to facilitate the political transition and prevent or contain the violence that its unwavering support of the dictatorship had helped to bring about (Kapteijns 2013). The famine that triggered the 1992 intervention was the aftermath of this violence. When the U.S. sent its military into Somalia in early December 1992, it had been formally absent from Somalia for less than two years. The film gives no inkling of this earlier involvement.

Third, while it was indeed U.S. Marines who landed on the beaches of Mogadishu in December 1992, they did so under the umbrella of a UN peacekeeping mission called Operation Restore Hope.[10] It is true that the U.S. was the politically and militarily dominant element, but this did not make the UN umbrella any less significant. The lack of clarity regarding this crucial dimension of the military intervention is not just an innocent form of filmic condensation, as becomes evident from the film's first action scene. As Aidiid's militias gun down civilians to claim a delivery of international food aid, the indignant TFR soldiers find themselves unable to intervene because of the restricted UN rules of engagement. This representation omits the history of UNOSOM I (United Nations Operations in Somalia I) and misrepresents the situation in October 1993. At the time of this UN/U.S. intervention in 1992, it was the UN that pushed for a restoration of security that would include disarmament of warlords on all sides of the conflict. However, Robert Oakley, the man President George Bush appointed as the U.S. Special Envoy to Somalia, actively resisted the explicitly stated objective of disarming warlords advocated by UN Secretary-General Boutros-Ghali, to the bewilderment and disappointment of many Somalis. Instead, Oakley 'cosied up' (de Waal 2008: 132) to General Aidiid and appears to have chosen him as the warlord with the most potential to win the civil war.[11] As de Waal (2008: 132) reports:

> Oakley rented his large and expensive residence in Mogadishu from Aidiid's main financier Osman 'Ato,' used Aidid's moneychangers for the lucrative business of converting U.S. dollars to Somali shillings,[12] and gave the general a series of public relations coups by heralding 'breakthroughs' in peace talks that had in fact been negotiated by UN diplomats some months earlier.

Oakley and his associates had therefore empowered the very warlord who was able to inflict such heavy losses on the U.S. military on 3 October 1993.[13] The film conceals – as Oakley has –- how U.S. policy contributed to making Aidiid more powerful than he had ever been. This was the situation in May 1993, at the beginning of a new stage of the UN/U.S. mission called UNOSOM II, which forms the background to the military operation of 3 October.[14]

Fourth and finally, the sparse narrative framing at the beginning of *Black Hawk Down* omits another important background factor, one that is relevant to understanding Somali attitudes towards U.S. soldiers on 3 October 1993. Ever since UNOSOM II had declared war on Aidiid, especially after the alleged murder and mutilation by Aidiid's militia of twenty-four UN peacekeepers on 6 June 1993, UN/U.S. military actions against him had claimed so many civilian lives that de Waal titled his essay 'U.S. War Crimes in Somalia' (2008). These incidents were known to the filmmakers, for they were described in the Bowden book on which the film was based. One of the worst incidents was that of 12 July 1993, during which U.S. Cobra helicopters attacked a meeting of politico-military leaders and elders of Aidiid's clan-based organization, who (it is now believed) had gathered to try to persuade Aidiid to negotiate a compromise with the UN. The aftermath left seventy-three men, women, and children dead and hundreds wounded (Bowden 2000: 73, 95).

One cannot expect the film to include all this information. However, it is important to note that its '*filmic* condensation' is in reality a '*mythic* condensation' that erases the long U.S. involvement in Somalia as well as the direct contributions of U.S. and UN policies to the violent situation in October 1993. The focus of the opening scene on the two innocent, caring young men of Task Force Ranger, Michael Durant (played by Ron Eldart) and Matt Eversmann (played by Josh Hartnett), therefore, serves as a displacement strategy that allows their horrified empathy to stand in for this history.

Somalis as Savage Foil for Mythically Enhanced U.S. Soldiers

Among the aspects of war films Mark Lacy (2003: 614–16) has categorized as conventional are an obsession with hypermasculinity, a 'libidinization of gadgets', and a process of 'abstractification' that distances viewers from the real harm war inflicts on human bodies. By these criteria, *Black Hawk Down* is only in part a conventional war film. For example, in the film's construction of masculinity, the hypermasculinity of Delta man 'Hoot' Gibson is balanced by the gentler, more social and idealist but equally attractive manliness of Eversmann. Lacy's 'libidinization of gadgets', the proverbial exhilaration of boys with toys, certainly seems relevant to *Black Hawk Down*'s fascination with military hardware, which filmmakers, actors, and the U.S. soldiers portrayed in the film appear to have shared (*BHD* 2003 2c). However, *Black Hawk Down* also shows how even the most sophisticated technology can fail – as when Black

Hawk combat helicopters are brought down by simple (though doctored) rocket-propelled grenades (Bowden 2000a: 110).

Black Hawk Down radically breaks with Lacy's definition of conventionality, however, in that it does not distance its viewers from what war and the tools of war do to human bodies. The film shows this in great and graphic detail in one scene after the other. A gunner is hit and, falling dead inside the vehicle, bleeds all over his comrades. One soldier has the lower part of his body shot off, another his thumb. Another U.S. soldier suddenly sees a severed hand, picks it up in a daze and puts it in his bag, while yet another is hit in such a way that the medic must thrust his fist into the wound to (vainly) try to clamp the artery. And so forth. This is part of the accuracy and immediacy the filmmakers wanted to create and of the excess of spectacle discussed above. It is therefore one of the central filmic strategies of *Black Hawk Down* to bring its viewers into moral proximity to war and to the U.S. soldiers who are bludgeoned by its effects.

The mythic or moral enhancement of the U.S. soldiers is at the heart of the film's project. In the course of writing his book Bowden developed an enormous empathy for the men who had survived Operation Irene. '[I]t was this approach to the matter,' he explained, 'that so intrigued Bruckheimer,' as well as Scott (Nolan 2002: 156; Burlas 2002).

A specific example of such mythic enhancement is the film's creation and juxtaposition of the two main characters portraying U.S. soldiers. Sergeant Matt Eversmann presents the unpretentious and kind-hearted Ranger, who sincerely believes in the mission of restoring hope to the Somalis. Delta Sergeant 'Hoot' Gibson is cast as a different kind of hero, namely a cynical (but no less dedicated) super soldier, who is emotionally self-contained and impatient of authority. It is not a problem that Eversmann did not recognize the liberalism or introspection attributed to him in the film (Lawrence and McGarrahan 2008: 455 *n.* 14) and the strategy to create the character of Hoot out of a 'fictionalized composite' of various U.S. soldiers, including the son-in-law of Delta Force's original founder, is common and acceptable (Nolan 2002: 158; Bowden 2000a: 206). What is significant to my argument is that these two constructions of moral manhood, which frame the youthful and innocent swagger of the other forty U.S. soldiers portrayed in the film, present a military masculinity that is totally moral – cocky, naïve and immature, perhaps, but always ethical and innocent. In *Black Hawk Down*, the men of Task Force Ranger bumble and bleed, but, thanks to their training and *esprit de corps* as well as force of circumstance, perform well and often heroically.[15]

However, the film's mythic enhancement of the characters representing the U.S. military relies on the mythic diminishment of those portraying Somalis as a savage 'other' who allows the heroic self of the U.S. military to shine all the more brightly.

There are only three significant Somali characters (with speaking parts) in the film, all based on real people, although none are played by Somali actors.[16] Yusuf Dahir Mo'allim (played by Razaaq Adoti) was one of the leaders of Aidiid's militia and, in the film, the man whose RPG (rocket-propelled grenade) brings down the first Black Hawk helicopter. Osman Ali 'Ato' (played by George W. Harris) was Aidiid's major financier and arms dealer. UNOSOM II briefly arrested him in the summer of 1993, an incident that is portrayed in the film. Abdullahi Hassan Firimbi (played by Treva Etienne) was pilot Mike Durant's captor during his eleven days as Aidiid's prisoner of war. In the film all three come across as intelligent and modern, and at least two of the three – Ato and Firimbi – also appear to be educated and middle class. Film viewers might potentially admire these men for outsmarting the Americans – Mo'allim because of his low-tech success against the high-tech enemy; Ato because he predicts that Task Force Ranger will not win and should not have come; and Firimbi because he treats Durant with some kindness. However, through the strategy of mythic diminishment, *Black Hawk Down* reduces the likelihood of such a positive reading.

Given the limited number of scenes that feature these three Somali characters, it is striking that the film nevertheless explicitly diminishes their moral qualities. In the case of the guerrilla fighter

Mo'allim, the opening scene of the film distances the viewers from him morally when he uses a huge machine gun to mow down civilians clamouring for a share of a food aid delivery. The moral of this is clear: this man is not just intent on killing American soldiers but his own innocent and unarmed fellow Somalis as well. Although Ato is, in many ways, well rendered as the smooth international criminal and arms dealer who resents the arrogance of U.S. power, the possibility that the audience might admire this smug and (in the film) strapping gangster is largely foreclosed when TFR Commander Major-General Garrison associates Ato during a brief interview with the word 'genocide' and the number of '300,000 dead and counting' (Nolan 2002: 7).[17] That Ato may well have been a CIA asset, whose arrest may have served to protect him as U.S. troops went after Aidiid, is not something the film raises as a possibility.[18]

Firimbi is the character with the most potential to win viewers' favour. However, in his case too the film makes an effective narrative intervention to prevent this and render him as totally 'other'. These are Firimbi's words to Durant:

> Do you really think if you get General Aidid, we will simply put down our weapons and adopt American Democracy? That the killing will stop? We know this: without victory there can be no peace. *There will always be killing, you see? This is how things are in our world.* (Nolan 2002: 102, my italics)

With these lines the film pushes Firimbi firmly back into the tribal world of ancient hatreds. In contrast, Durant's perception of Firimbi during their eleven days together was more ambiguous and complex. Durant realized that he was a pawn in a 'high-stakes game of international poker', whose players were sophisticated negotiators. He wrote, 'The might of America strained at its leash just outside my prison, while these Third World "primitives" who were holding me were as savvy as a New York PR firm, knowing exactly how to manipulate the media and use me for their ends' (Durant 2003: 317).[19] However, nothing in his briefings about Somalia had prepared Durant for what he witnessed at the time of his release. It was Firimbi who drove with him to the U.N. compound in the western part of Mogadishu to hand him over. As they approached the gate, Firimbi 'flashed a bona fide set of UN credentials,' Durant wrote, not able to believe his eyes: 'Firimbi's wearing a "Viva Aidid" T-shirt, which is like waving a sign saying "I'm the Enemy". But he's got UN credentials!? It was the final bit of absurdity in a totally screwed-up world'. Never during his stay in Somalia, he noted, had he ever felt such a 'babe in the woods' (2003: 338).

Even if Bowden and the filmmakers did not know this part of Durant's story – which cannot be automatically assumed – the point is that the film not only dumbs down Somali characters such as Firimbi but also reduces Somali–U.S./UN relations to a simple and simplistic binary. The moral diminishment of the Somali characters is so absolute that it precludes even the possibility that the lines between good and evil, innocence and guilt, intelligent intent and tribal instinct, and modernity and backwardness might not be so clear-cut. The result is a serious misrepresentation of the historical moment the film set out to portray.

It is, however, in how the film casts the 1,100 or so other Somali characters, the extras, that its mythic diminishment of the Somalis is most extreme. First of all, apart from the character of the Somali spy, there is no evidence of any ethnically Somali actor in the whole film. How did this happen? In the film script, William J. Dowd, responsible for engaging the extras, explained this as follows: 'Since there are few, if any, Somalis living in Morocco ... we had to organize people from some 30 other countries in Africa who are working or studying in and around Rabat' (Nolan 2002: 160). As a result, the individuals who make up the various Somali mobs in the film consist of nationals from Angola, Burkina Faso, Congo, Djibouti, Ghana, Nigeria, Sierra Leone and Senegal, as well as 'Moroccans and Berbers from the southern deserts, of sub-Saharan descent' (ibid.). Of these 1,100, fifty men received training as stuntmen so that they could portray Somali militia men. However, even these do not stand out in the crowd, for the absence of any individual characterization of the Somalis in the film (beyond the three characters referred to above) is nearly absolute. No wonder that, on the few occasions that

Black Hawk Down: Recasting U.S. Military History

the Somali language is spoken in the film, this largely takes the form of brief, poorly pronounced, if not savagely screamed, imperatives and exclamations.

One cannot but conclude that Scott and Bruckheimer, who, in the name of 'making it real', spared no effort to import a whole section of the U.S. military into Morocco, were completely uninterested in such realism when it came to the Somali dimension of the film. The film's rendering of the Somalis as an undifferentiated, generically Black, violent mob is a strategy that creates enormous moral distance between them and the film's audience (see Introduction, Hoffman, Eltringham, this volume, for a discussion of Africans as a 'frantic mass'). It is a portrayal, as one film critic put it, that 'converts the Somalis into a pack of snarling dark-skinned beasts' (Mitchell 2001) running amok in a city that is 'beyond control, a wild zone, a space of otherness' (Lacy 2003: 619) or, as the U.S. soldiers often called it, 'a bad place' and 'pure Indian territory' (Bolger 1995: 314; Lawrence and McGarrahan 2008: 450). In the film the Somalis are rendered so anonymously that Mogadishu itself becomes the enemy (see Hoffman, this volume, for a discussion of the image of the violent African city).

Another strategy the film uses to morally distance and diminish its Somali characters is its failure to represent the impact of the violence of war on *Somali* bodies in the same way that it graphically shows the effect on *American* bodies. Although Somalis are mowed down in large numbers throughout the film,[20] they resemble figures in a video game[21] whose physical and psychological suffering is almost completely erased. Yet, as is evident from Bowden's interviews, some of the U.S. soldiers had very specific and at times traumatic memories of this suffering. Specialist Shawn Nelson described how a Somali woman who ran across the street with a basket full of RPGs was slowly shot to pieces in three successive volleys of U.S. fire. When he first saw her, he saw a woman whose blue dress was billowing out behind her. The first volley blew off her legs and left her 'a bloody lump', while the second caused her body to come further apart. After the third, he said, 'the woman no longer even looked like a human being; she'd been transformed into a monstrous bleeding hulk, like someone from a horror movie' (Bowden 2000a: 217–18). Another soldier described what ensued when a Little Bird helicopter strafed a group of Somalis with machine gun fire: 'A Little Bird swooped in and threw a flaming wall of lead over at it. Those who didn't fall, fled. One moment there was a crowd, and the next instant it was just a bleeding heap of dead and injured' (Bowden 1997). Add to this how the film script (Nolan 2002: 113) describes a similar scene, this time from the perspective of a Little Bird pilot who is about to strafe the street and rooftops close to where the Black Hawks and their crews (here called 'chalks') had gone down and where the U.S. soldiers were pinned down overnight:

> He sees THOUSANDS of glowing Somali bodies, ghostly, innumerable on his infra-red monitor.
>
> ADJOINING ROOFTOPS – more than 200 heat signatures of Somali bodies charge across rooftops coming towards the chalks in a great wave, leaping from roof to roof.
>
> OPPOSITE SIDE OF THE STREET – Three hundred Somalis move to get in position to fire down at the chalks. Somalis climb up stairs and ladders, appearing on rooftops *like angry insects*. [my italics].

The moral distancing of Somalis produced by the film, therefore, exceeds even that of the soldiers who actually faced Somalis in the battle of 3 October. Though most of the latter used pejorative names for the Somalis (Skinnies, Sammies, Indians, and worse), several also expressed admiration for the latter's skills as urban guerrilla fighters – their discipline and determination – and not just stunned bewilderment at their seemingly mad courage (Bowden 2000a: 117, 125, 234).

The one significant exception to the lack of individual characterization of Somalis is the scene that poignantly renders the utter desolation of what appears to be a Somali non-combatant. As the UN rescue convoy in the early morning of 4 October finally begins to exit the war zone, an old man, carrying the lifeless body of a young child in his arms, crosses in front of the vehicles in a rain

Black Hawk Down: Recasting U.S. Military History

of bullets to which he is oblivious. This is a powerful moment of filmic condensation and, to my mind, virtually the only scene that does not morally diminish the film's Somali characters.[22] But, it is immediately balanced by another rare moment of individual characterization, a powerfully negative one. This scene shows a Somali woman with a child in her arms who, as a U.S. soldier watches her incredulously and holds his fire, suddenly points a gun at him while shouting a Somali profanity. The soldier kills her before she can shoot. Overall, *Black Hawk Down* insists, Somali civilians are neither peaceful nor innocent.

On the U.S. side, however, the film repeatedly shows how commanders and soldiers remind each other of the rules of engagement – only shoot those who shoot at you – even though Operation Irene, as a Special Forces operation, had its own protocol. Its U.S. participants do not mention such reminders. There is no doubt that Somali women and children participated in the fighting on 3 October, minimally as spotters, but many were simply caught in the crossfire and happened to be in the wrong place at the wrong time. As Lawrence and McGarrahan (2008: 444) note, the Somalis 'undergo a mythic diminishment that renders them as embodiments of tribal primitivism, warlordism, and cynicism about the death of their own people and as suicidal in battle'.

From the many comments the filmmakers have made on their film, it becomes clear how little they knew and cared to know about the Somalis.[23] Even the well-intentioned Bowden, who in preparation of his book made a special trip to Mogadishu, could not overcome the radical 'othering' of the Somalis that also characterizes the film. This is how he connects their urban guerrilla tactics to their tribal or clan identity:

> Somalis were famous for braving enemy fire, for almost suicidal, frontal assaults. They were brought up in clans and named for their fathers and grandfathers. They entered the fight with cunning and courage and gave themselves over to the savage emotion of it. Retreat, even before overwhelming fire, was considered unmanly. For the clan, they were always ready to die. (Bowden 2000a: 110)[24]

57

The view of Somalis as savage tribesmen living under the violent dictate of their custom thus shaped the film from its very conception. In expressing the dramatic tension of the film in music, Hans Zimmer (2002), the composer responsible for the sound track of *Black Hawk Down*, approaches the film score from the same premise:

> I wanted the music to portray two tribes ... One was the techno tribe, which is America. They have all the technology. The other tribe is the ethnic instruments, which is the Somali world. These two tribes collide, and music is what shows the gulf between the two cultures.

Thus Zimmer's music weaves back and forth between 'world music' (exemplified by the Senegalese bard Baaba Maal and the Algerian singer Rachid Taha) to accompany the Somali scenes; techno music with driving military drums and Moroccan percussion for the battle scenes; and a range of Western music, from orchestral symphony to folk ballad, for the scenes with the Americans. To this writer's mind, the result is powerful and beautiful, as the representatives of the so-called world music hold their own and are not overwhelmed by the other genres (*BHD* 2003 2d). While he also regards the Somalis as 'other', Zimmer's representation is not so negative as to force listeners into an attitude of moral indifference. This is a significant achievement.

However, one question nevertheless presents itself: why completely ignore – beyond the two fragments of love song briefly audible in the Somali spy's car – modern Somali music and popular song, so abundant for the period relevant to the film (see Kapteijns 2009, 2010; Kapteijns and Omar Ali 1999). Given how the film either caricatures or erases all Somali cultural specificity, the failure to include (or look for inspiration from) Somali music thus conforms, and fails to provide an antidote, to the film's overall diminishment of the Somalis.

In the end, no one, not even the well-intentioned composer, has any interest in rendering Somalis in *Black Hawk Down* with the same accuracy, immediacy and moral proximity to which they aspire in their representation of the U.S. military men. The film's Somalis are incidental to the film beyond providing a savage foil for the fallible but heroic men of Task Force Ranger. This is why the filmmakers do not need to have knowledge about them or portray them realistically or accurately. In the film, therefore, as Lacy (2003: 619) puts it, 'Mogadishu becomes a fantasy place where men from the most powerful state in the world confront a temporary breakdown in their supremacy ... and attempt to gain control, order and "omnipotence"'.

Recasting Military Defeat as Victory: Political Implications after 9/11

Through the strategies of mythic condensation and plain misrepresentation, the film also provides closure to the narrative about 3 October and recasts the U.S. parties involved in ways that have specific political implications. These misrepresentations do not foreclose multiple political responses to the film, but limit the range of possibility and thus advance 'preferred readings' about the role of the U.S. and the U.S. military in the world.

One of the intentional misrepresentations of the U.S. side of the story includes the mythic enhancement of the TFR commanders at the expense of the lower ranks; the near concealment (or mythic condensation) of the humiliating violations and mutilations of the TFR soldiers who were killed in battle, and the sparse but politically charged filmic condensation in the framing of the film's end. Together these strategies recast the disastrous outcome of Operation Irene as a military victory and boost the reputation of the U.S. military. Moreover, in the context of the post 9/11 political climate, these strategies enable a 'preferred reading' by which viewers embrace U.S. military intervention as the arduous but moral and necessary task of heroic men.

Black Hawk Down does not completely whitewash command failures,[25] but, as Lawrence and McGarrahan (2008: 440–41) have shown, small inaccuracies in the attribution of responsibility for mistakes made during Operation Irene incorrectly shift the blame away from the military commanders and onto the common soldiers. Similarly, the film transfers credit for what it renders as good and noble decisions – such as the command to leave no man behind – up the line of command to TFR's top commander, General Garrison (ibid., 447–48). Moreover, beyond casual negative references to Clinton and 'Washington', the film never even hints at General Garrison's superiors, protecting *them* from blame even more effectively.

A second strategic misrepresentation of the U.S. side of the story of 3 October is the underrepresentation and concealment of its most humiliating aspects. Back in 1993, the incidents and images that had defined Operation Irene as a humiliating defeat in the eyes of the American public were the televised violations of American soldiers' bodies dragged through the streets of Mogadishu. These images were, therefore, a challenge to the film's suggestion that the mission was a success and that the U.S. soldiers had behaved heroically. *Black Hawk Down* does not conceal the fact that some men had been left behind when the rescue convoy reached safety in the early morning of 4 October, but nevertheless misrepresents this situation in two important ways.

First, it omits and conceals the fact that the captured Durant and the dead bodies of six other U.S. soldiers were retrieved as a result of U.S. *political*, not *military* intervention. Second, it only gestures at the humiliation U.S. soldiers experienced at Somali hands when their bodies were mutilated and dragged through the streets. These events are condensed into a very brief scene during which Durant, with bare torso, is hoisted onto the shoulders of a Somali mob. The filmmakers may well have taken this decision out of respect for the dead soldiers and their families, but this omission nevertheless belies the documentary-like accuracy and realism they claimed for the film and conceals those aspects that would have been the greatest obstacle to presenting Operation Irene as a military success. As Sergeant Jeff Struecker wrote in his account of the event, the bodies of the soldiers who had been killed began to be dropped off at the gate of the U.S. military compound only after Robert Oakley had been brought back to negotiate with Aidiid. One body appeared without its head, which was delivered later, after more negotiations. Some of the bodies had already been buried. 'We saw up close how brutally some of our comrades had been mutilated,' Struecker wrote, adding that '[s]ome of the bodies were so battered they could not be identified until they reached Dover Air Force Base in Delaware, where dental records and other information were available' (2006: 132).[26] Given that these very events had turned Operation Irene into a military defeat in the eyes of the U.S. public in 1993, omitting them was not a neutral but a political act. In fact, it was an act of alchemy in which Hollywood magic transformed defeat into victory.

The reception of the film by the U.S. military is in this respect telling. General John M. Keane, the U.S. Army's Vice-Chief of Staff, remembered that Bruckheimer had promised him that he would make a film of which the Army would be proud. 'He did, so we thank him for it,' the General reportedly said (Lawrence and McGarrahan 2008: 431). On 15 January 2001, a special gala screening of *Black Hawk Down* was held in Washington, DC, attended by top-ranking military and civilian representatives of the U.S. Department of Defence, including Vice-President Dick Cheney, Defence Secretary Donald Rumsfeld and Deputy Defence Secretary Paul Wolfowitz (ibid.: 432). Joe Burlas (2002) reported on the speech that director Ridley Scott gave on this occasion:

> [T]hat he and co-producer Jerry Bruckheimer decided to make the movie to set the record straight. He said there was an apparent public misperception that the military messed up in Somalia, when in fact it was heroic in a very unstable part of the world. 'We thought those soldiers should be remembered for their courage'.

By hitching the courage of the soldiers of Task Force Ranger to the prestige of the U.S. military as a whole and the retrieval of 3 October as a victory, this final phrase, like the film, indeed constitutes, as Lawrence and McGarrahan (2008: 440) have also argued, a perfect displacement strategy.

The top officials who attended this gala screening were closely associated with the administration of President George W. Bush, whose father had initiated the military intervention in Somalia in

1992 and who was now himself at war in Afghanistan as part of his overall 'war on terror'. They had reason to be pleased with the film even beyond the way it rescued the reputation of Task Force Ranger in Operation Irene. This brings us back to the third and last strategy of misrepresentation whose political implications must be discussed, namely the sparse framing of the film's end.

Black Hawk Down concludes with a series of short texts to which the film script refers as 'legends' (Nolan 2002: 128–29). The first legend opens by stating the casualties of 3 October: 'over 1,000 Somalis died and 19 U.S. soldiers lost their lives' (Nolan 2002: 128).[27] It then scrolls the names of the nineteen soldiers who lost their lives during Operation Irene and presents the text of the note Sergeant Ruiz had prepared for his wife and children in case he would not survive. The second consists of three brief statements, that two Delta sergeants received posthumous medals of honour; that 'Michael Durant was released after 11 days of captivity'; and that '[t]wo weeks later, President Clinton withdrew Delta Force and The Rangers from Somalia' (Nolan 2002: 128).

This filmic condensation of the aftermath of Operation Irene pays a brief but emotional tribute to the soldiers killed in the battle and blames President Clinton for hastily withdrawing Task Force Ranger from Mogadishu. By creating an emotional bond between viewers and the U.S. soldiers, especially those who were killed in battle on 3 October, and by emphasizing U.S. political failure (troop withdrawal) instead of military miscalculation and disaster, the film enables a reading that Operation Irene was a military success and diverts attention away from military command failures to love and admiration for the Task Force soldiers.

This interpretation, which, as was shown above, both filmmakers and top U.S. military leaders enthusiastically and publicly embraced, was also the major political message conveyed by the film's military advisers, some of the men portrayed in the film, and even the actors. All strongly insisted that, from a military and tactical perspective, Operation Irene was a successful mission (*BHD* 2003 3a).

This same group of men, however, expressed different opinions about the limits of what military force and war could and should try to accomplish, especially, as some actors put it, in a limited timeframe and in places like Somalia where 'the fight has been going on for thousands of years' (*BHD* 2003 2e; Bolger 1995: x). Here the filmmakers differed, at least at the time of the film's release. Then they articulated publicly and explicitly that, especially given what happened after 11 September 2001, U.S. military intervention was a political duty the U.S. could not shrink; war might be dirty work, but someone had to do it.

Most explicit about the political implications of *Black Hawk Down* is Bowden's description of how the 'end crawl', as these closing lines are also called, came about. He recounted how Scott and Bruckheimer had asked him to connect the events of 3 October 1993 to those of December 2001, the date of the film's release, when the U.S. was at war in Afghanistan. He wrote:

> We all felt … that the Mogadishu battle had prompted not just a sudden end to the mission in Somalia, but a withdrawal of American military force from the world. The world paid a terrible price for that – in Rwanda, Bosnia, and Kosovo. Even the attacks in New York and Washington were connected in that the Clinton administration had not forcefully gone after Osama bin Laden and al-Qaeda after the 1999 bombings of U.S. embassies in Kenya and Tanzania. (Bowden 2002: xv)[28]

Scott himself also commented explicitly on the political implications of *Black Hawk Down*. He connected it to 9/11 and its aftermath in slightly different terms, making two separate arguments, both relevant to the military intervention in Somalia. To his mind, U.S. military intervention in humanitarian disasters in the world was an unavoidable moral and political necessity. Extending this argument, he argued that the changes that became undeniably obvious on 9/11 had already been at work in 1993: 'And the lesson is that if you don't watch the back door, somebody will come through it' (Nolan 2002: 175). In other words, the U.S. was not necessarily wrong in having intervened in Somalia, but its hurried withdrawal from Mogadishu meant that it had not watched the world's back door – and al-Qaeda had walked right through it. Indeed, between 1992 and May 1996, Osama bin Laden had headquartered his *mujahidin* movement in the Sudan and Somalis appear to have been involved in the al-Qaeda-related bombings of the U.S. embassies in Kenya and Tanzania in August 1998. Bowden's book, first published in 1999, does contain a reference to the presence in Somalia of foreign *mujahidin* helping to train Aidiid's militia, describing them as 'Islamic soldiers smuggled in from Sudan, who had experience fighting Soviet helicopters in Afghanistan' (2000a: 110). The film, however, makes no reference to such soldiers or the role of Islamist politics and motivations on the side of the Somalis. This lack of reference suggests that there is a gap between the political messages enabled by the film itself, which had been conceived and produced before 11 September 2001, and those the film's makers publicly articulated at the time of its release in December 2001.

This calls for a comparison of the answers the film and its makers present to the two questions asked by Scott: first, whether Somalis and people like them deserve U.S. military intervention and are capable of benefiting from it and, second, whether Somalis in 1993 presented the backdoor by which al-Qaeda entered the world with, as outcome, the attacks of 9/11. The *film* appears to answer both these questions negatively. To begin with the first, it opens by introducing the U.S. military intervention as a humanitarian one that had been completed successfully. It then presents the operation of 3 October as occurring in a new stage of this mission, when Aidiid began to attack and kill U.S. and UN soldiers. In this new phase, the film suggests, Somalis no longer consisted of brutal warlords and innocent civilian victims but were aggressive and ungrateful Third World wretches towards whom moral indifference is fully justified.

This portrayal is in complete accord with the conclusion Bowden drew in his book. The Somalis blew the opportunity the UN/U.S. interventions had presented, Bowden (2000a: 334) wrote, and as a result 'the great ship of international goodwill' had sailed. He concluded: 'Rightly or wrongly, they stand as an enduring symbol of Third World ingratitude and intractability, of the futility of trying to resolve local animosity with international muscle. They've effectively written themselves off the map' (2000a: 334).

This leaves Scott's second question. Does the film present Somalia in 1993 as a breeding ground for al-Qaeda or is this the political interpretation put on it by its makers after its release? If one focuses only on the film's portrayal of Somalis, there is no reason to see them as a danger outside the tribal 'wild zone' of their 'otherness', in which their fury against the Western outsiders remains incomprehensible and appears non-specific (Lacy 2003: 620). However, there are other aspects of the film that viewers, in the context of its release, could harness to patriotic support for the war against terror and the invasion of Afghanistan. I will briefly summarize these by way of conclusion.

These are the aspects of the film that, in the context of December 2001 and an America again at war, enabled readings of the film as pro-war and pro-U.S. military intervention. First of all, the film retrieves 3 October 1993 as a military success and, through an array of filmic strategies, becomes a tribute to the U.S. military and the universal U.S. soldier. In its opening scenes, *Black Hawk Down*, moreover, supports the initial U.S. (and UN) military intervention under President Bush, while its 'end crawl' suggests that it was President Clinton who was to blame for withdrawing the U.S. soldiers before they could finish the job. *Black Hawk Down* may not distance viewers of the film from the horrors of war and what it does to the bodies of U.S. soldiers, but it enables a 'preferred reading' that war is necessary and that fighting (and occasionally dying) for the cause is the messy but noble work U.S. soldiers do and do well. And finally, the film renders Third World 'others' like the Somalis as incidental and morally irrelevant to this necessary work.

In the context of December 2001, not just viewers but also the filmmakers and important representatives of the U.S. military were able to draw these aspects out and directly connect them to the film. Thus, Bowden and Scott explicitly connected Somalia 1993 with al-Qaeda and 9/11. Thus, defence luminaries enthusiastically and publicly embraced the film. Thus, commercial interests tried to

65

cash in on the connection between the film and the new war, with Revolution Studios deciding to bring the release of the film forward in time from March 2002 to Christmas 2001 (Bowden 2002: xv) and a Sony representative claiming that the war in Afghanistan was very relevant to the film and, one assumes, its box office innings.[29] In the U.K., those who pre-ordered the film's DVD edition, received 'dog tags' of the soldiers killed on 3 October as mementos. This assumed and reaffirmed the idea, as Lacy (2003: 621) argues, 'that the viewer shares the same moral and political geography of the U.S. soldiers'.

That a careful reading of the film's portrayal of Somalis and Somalia, as I argue above, does *not* yield any hints that the Somalia of 1993 was a back door for worldwide terrorism or that Somalis were a threat beyond the 'Indian country' of Aidiid's Bakkara Market neighbourhood, only underlines how incidental and irrelevant Somalis are to the film. This is ironic, for one may argue that the military operation of 3 October 1993 failed because the U.S. soldiers were not knowledgeable enough about the Somalis and did not take them seriously enough; this caused them to underestimate Somali capabilities as well as the depth of their suffering and humiliation at the hands of the intervention forces.

This is how pilot Durant puts it at the end of his book: 'In general, my emphasis is never to underestimate the enemy's capability or willingness to fight' (2003: 357). If it had been up to Somali-Canadian free verse poet Mohamud S. Togane, the film's tag line of the film would not have been 'Leave no man behind', but the Somali proverb 'Ragow, kibirka waa lagu kufaa, kaas ha la ogaado'. In Togane's translation and annotation for the occasion, this means:

> O men, pride brings disaster. Especially your silly selfish solipsistic Yankee clannish pride in the pitiless pedigree of honkydom! Let that be remembered. Let that be known. Pride must have a fall. Pride goes before destruction. A haughty spirit before a fall. Let that be remembered. Let that be known'.[30]

Notes

1. The operation was carried out by Rangers and Delta soldiers of the U.S. Task Force Ranger (TFR). See Bolger (1995: 314–15).
2. Especially Lacy (2003), Lisle and Pepper (2005) and Lawrence and McGarrahan (2008).
3. See Lisle and Pepper (2005: 179–80) and McCrisken and Pepper (2005: 189).
4. Lisle and Pepper (2005: 171) derive the concept of 'preferred readings' (interpretations conforming to existing power relations) from Stuart Hall.
5. For these concepts, see Lawrence and McGarrahan (2008: 439 *ff.*) and Lacy (2002: 620).
6. For the concept of 'moral proximity', see Lacy (2003: 632).
7. For the concept of 'mythic condensation', see Lawrence and McGarrahan (2008: 439, 443–45).
8. For further analysis, see Kapteijns 2010 and Kapteijns 2013.
9. For background, see Blumenthal (1993) and Clarke and Herbst (1997). Hirsch and Oakley (1995) and Bolton (2004) are biased, while Bolger (1995) is valuable for the military aspect.
10. Operating under UN Chapter VII, this intervention was called UNITAF from 3 December 1992 to 4 May 1993 and UNOSOM I from 27 April 1992 to 4 May 1993. From then, the mission came to be called UNOSOM II, which had state-building objectives, also under UN Chapter VII, and less U.S. troop involvement. U.S. Task Force Ranger was sent to Somalia in August 1993 in the context of the latter. See Clarke (1993) and Bolger (1995).
11. Oakley (1995: 16) has incorrectly claimed neutrality. For further analysis of the different stages of military humanitarian intervention in Somalia, see Kapteijns, "Test-firing the 'New World Order' in Somalia: The U.S./UN Military Humanitarian Intervention of 1992–1995," submitted to the *Journal of Genocide Research*.
12. This practice continued, de Waal argues, throughout the war, even when Aidiid became the target of the UN/U.S. forces in Somalia.
13. In March 1993 Oakley had declared the mission 'largely accomplished' and 'the problem of clan warfare ... virtually gone' (Blumenthal 1993: 58).
14. The command structure of Operation Gothic Serpent, of which Operation Irene was a part, was highly complex. According to Bolger (1995: 308–10), there were one UN and two U.S. chains of command in Mogadishu at the time, while Garrison also had a 'direct stove pipe' into the White House.
15. For other examples of mythic enhancement, see Struecker (2006: 121).
16. A further minor character is the Somali spy.
17. In a BBC interview, Ato complained about his portrayal in the film

('Warlord thumbs down' BBC News, Tuesday, 29 January 2002. Retrieved on 18 February 2011 from http://news.bbc.co.uk/2/hi/africa/1789170.stm).
18. This is suggested by Ato's close connections to the American oil company Conoco, and Oakley, and is a belief held by many Somalis.
19. The public version of the negotiations that led to Durant's release is that Oakley, brought back to Somalia for that purpose, met face-to-face with Aidiid and threatened him. However, it was Aidiid who took the initiative and ensured that the hunt for him was called off and the Somalis captured during Operation Irene were released (Bowden 2000a: 326).
20. For the number of rockets and amounts of ammunition fired by the U.S. soldiers during certain episodes of Operation Irene see de Waal (2008: 131) and Bolger (1995: 322).
21. For Novalogic's video game *Delta Force: Black Hawk Down*, see Lawrence and McGarrahan (2008: 450).
22. A negative reading interprets the elderly Somali as displaying an un-Islamic disregard for life by neglecting even to cover the small corpse he is taking for burial.
23. For the ignorance of Somali geography and history displayed by executive producer Branko Lustig and production designer Arthur Max, see Nolan (2002: 168).
24. If one rereads this passage while substituting the words 'American soldiers' for 'Somalis' and 'nation' for 'clan', it yields a positive description of U.S. soldiers.
25. See Nolan (2002: 83) for the problems with guiding the convoy from the air.
26. Similarly, the film omits that Durant, as he lay wounded outside his crashed helicopter, was hit in the face with the severed arm of one of his fallen comrades (Durant 2003: 43) and that the only way the U.S. soldiers could dislodge the corpse of one of the pilots of the second downed helicopter was by pulling the body apart (Struecker 2006: 116).
27. There are no reliable estimates of Somali casualties for the battle of 3 October but see Alford (2010: 48), de Waal (2008: 142), Bowden (2000a: 310), and Schmitt (1993). The U.S. soldiers themselves (Bowden 2000a and *BHD* 2003 3a) speak of Somalis dying by the hundreds and describe how it seemed like all of Mogadishu had died, that it was like doomsday.
28. In the end, the filmmakers decided to 'leave such connections to the viewers' imagination' (Bowden 2002: xv).
29. For responses by viewers who interpreted the film as pro-military, see Bowden 2002 and www.bbc.co.uk/films/2002/01/10/josh_harnett_black_hawk_down_2002_interview.shtml, accessed 17 February 2011.
30. This is from a poem called 'Black Hawk Down' Togane sent to the author on 27 January 2011 in response to the query whether he had written about the film. Other analysts have spoken about the U.S. military failure

of 3 October in the similar terms of 'victory disease' (Lacy 2003: 436) and 'the sin of pride' (Bolger 1995: 330).

Filmography

Scott, R. (Dir.) 2001. *Black Hawk Down* (Revolution Studios, Jerry Bruckheimer Films).
Scott, R. (Dir.) 2003. *Black Hawk Down: Leave No Man Behind*, 3-Disc Deluxe Edition. Culver City, CA: Columbia Tristar Home Entertainment.
BHD 2003 (1) Disc One: *Black Hawk Down* 2001, directed by Ridley Scott and produced by Jerry Bruckheimer (Revolution Studios, Jerry Bruckheimer Films).
BHD 2003 (2) Disc Two: *The Essence of Combat: Making Black Hawk Down*: (a) 'Getting it Right'; (b) 'Crash Course'; (c) 'Battlefield Morocco'; (d) 'Hymn to the Fallen'; (e) 'After Action Report'.
BHD 2003 (3) Disc Three: (a) The History Channel 2002. 'The True Story of Black Hawk Down', 21 January 2002; (b) PBS, Frontline 1998. 'Ambush in Mogadishu', written, produced and directed by William Cran.

References

Alford, M. 2010. *Reel Power: Hollywood Cinema and American Supremacy*. London: Pluto Press.
Blumenthal, S. 1993. 'Why Are We in Somalia?', *The New Yorker*, 25 October.
Bolger, D.P. 1995. *Savage Peace: Americans at War in the 1990s*. Novato, CA: Presidio.
Bolton, J.R. 2004. 'Wrong Turn in Somalia', *Foreign Affairs* 73(1): 56–66.
Bowden, M. 1997. 'Helicopter Provides Support', *The Arizona Republic*, 24 December.
Bowden, M. 2000a. *Black Hawk Down: A Story of Modern War*. Harmondsworth: Penguin.
Bowden, M. 2000b. 'Narrative Journalism Goes Multimedia', Nieman Foundation for Journalism at Harvard University. Retrieved on 13 January 2011 from http://www.nieman.harvard.edu/reportsitemprint.aspx?id=101578
Bowden, M. 2002. 'Foreword', in K. Nolan (ed.), *Black Hawk Down: The Shooting Script*. New York: Newmarket Press, pp. vii–xv.
Brons, M.H. 2001. *Society, Security, Sovereignty and the State. Somalia: from Statelessness to Statelessness?* Utrecht: International Books.
Burlas, J. 2002. '*Black Hawk Down* reflects Army values', reporting for the Army News Service, 17 January. Retrieved on 2 March 2011 from http://forum.keypublishing.co.uk/archive/index.php?t-4385.html

Clarke, W. 1993. 'Testing the World's Resolve in Somalia', *Parameters: Journal of the U.S. Army War College* 4(23): 12–58.
Clarke, W. and J. Herbst (eds). 1997. *Learning from Somalia: The Lessons of Armed Humanitarian Intervention*. Boulder, CO: Westview Press.
de Waal, A. de. 2008. 'U.S. War Crimes in Somalia', *New Left Review* I(230): 131–44.
Durant, M.J. 2003. *In the Company of Heroes*. New York: Putnam.
Foden, G. 2002. 'You can't diddle with the truth', *The Guardian*, 11 January.
Gross, T. 2005. 'Ridley Scott Discusses Making His Oscar-Nominated Movie *Black Hawk Down*', in L.E. Knapp and A.F. Kulas (eds), *Ridley Scott Interviews*. Jackson: University of Missisippi, pp. 206–17.
Hirsch, J. and R.B. Oakley 1995. *Somalia and Operation Restore Hope: Reflections on Peacemaking and Peacekeeping*. Washington, DC: United States Institute of Peace Press.
Kapteijns, L. 2009. 'Discourse on Moral Womanhood in Somali Popular Songs, 1960–1990', *Journal of African History* 50(1): 101–122.
Kapteijns, L. 2010. 'Making Memories of Mogadishu in Somali Poetry about the Civil War', in L. Kapteijns and A. Richters (eds), *Mediations of Violence in Africa: Fashioning New Futures from Contested Pasts*. Leiden: Brill, pp. 25–74.
Kapteijns, L. 2013. *Clan Cleansing in Somalia: The Ruinous Legacy of 1991*. Philadelphia: University of Pennsylvania Press.
Kapteijns, L. with Maryan Omar Ali. 1999. *Women's Voices in a Man's World: Women and the Pastoral Tradition in Northern Somali Orature, c. 1899–1980*. Portsmouth, NH: Heinemann.
Lacy, M.J. 2003. 'War, Cinema, and Moral Anxiety', *Alternatives* 28(5): 611–36.
Lawrence, J.S. and J.G. McGarrahan. 2008. 'Operation Restore Honor in *Black Hawk Down*', in P.C. Rollins and J.E. O'Connor (eds), *Why We Fought: America's Wars in Film and History*. Lexington: University of Kentucky Press, pp. 431–57.
Lisle, D. and A. Pepper. 2005. 'The New Face of Global Hollywood: *Black Hawk Down* and the Politics of Meta-Sovereignty', *Cultural Politics* 1(2): 165–92.
Maren, M. 1997. *The Road to Hell: The Ravaging Effects of Foreign Aid and International Charity*. New York: The Free Press.
McCrisken, T. and A. Pepper. 2005. *American History and Contemporary Hollywood Film*. New Brunswick, NJ: Rutgers University Press.
Mitchell, E. 2001. 'Film Review: Mission of Mercy Goes Bad in Africa', *The New York Times*, 28 December.
Nolan, K. 2002. *Black Hawk Down: The Shooting Script*. New York: Newmarket Press.
Oakley, R. 1995. 'Imposing Values: An Ambassador Looks Back at Mogadishu', *WorldView*, Winter: 13–19.

Rawson, D. 1994. 'Dealing with Disintegration: U.S. Assistance and the Somali State', in A.I. Samatar (ed.), *The Somali Challenge: From Catastrophe to Renewal?* Boulder, CO: Lynne Rienner, pp. 147–87.
Schmitt, E. 1993. 'Somali War Casualties May Be 10,000', *The New York Times*, 8 December.
Springer, C. 1988. 'Antiwar Film as Spectacle: Contradictions in the Combat Sequence', *Genre* 21(4): 479–86.
Struecker, J. with Dean Merrill. 2006. *The Road to Unafraid: How the Army's Top Rangers Faced Fear and Found Courage through* Black Hawk Down *and Beyond*. Nashville, Tennessee: W Publishing Group.
Zimmer, H., P. Scalia, and B. Badami. 2002. *Black Hawk Down: Original Music Soundtrack*. Decca, UMG Sound Tracks.

Three

Pharma in Africa
Health, Corruption and Contemporary Kenya in *The Constant Gardener*

Daniel Branch

Introduction

The end of the Cold War posed a mighty challenge to its great storyteller. Between the lines of accounts of the fall of the Berlin Wall and the collapse of the Soviet Union, John le Carré could, in his own words, 'read my own obituary'. He had little choice but to become 'the spy novelist who came in from the Cold War' (Gussow 2000). Although his attention shifted away from the intrigues of the Cold War, le Carré's willingness to tackle the big issues of the day was undimmed. In the afterword to a new edition of *The Secret Pilgrim*, he writes, 'Now that the West had dealt with rogue forms of Communism, I wanted to ask, how was it going to deal with rogue forms of capitalism?' *The Constant Gardener* is meant to provide an answer (2011: 408).

The novel (2001) and Jeffrey Caine's adaption (2005) depict a world in which the interests of multinationals have supplanted those of nation states as the driving force behind international diplomacy. The British government is shown as complicit in the cover-up of the murder of Tessa Quayle (Rachel Weisz) and her Belgian-Congolese colleague, Arnold Bluhm (Hubert Koundé), in northern Kenya. The two are murdered in an effort to prevent them from publicizing the details of a botched trial of a new drug 'Dypraxa'. The trial of the treatment for tuberculosis, produced by KDH and tested in Kenya by Three Bees (both fictional companies), results in the deaths of many of its subjects. Surrounded by colleagues complicit in the establishment of the fatally flawed Dypraxa trial and the sabotaging of the police investigation, the film follows Tessa's widower, Justin Quayle (Ralph Fiennes), a diplomat at the British High Commission in Nairobi, as he seeks to find the truth about his wife's murder.

By virtue of its subject matter and of its Brazilian director, Fernando Meirelles, *The Constant Gardener* promised to be an innovative addition to the films made about Kenya and its people. From the sub-genre of Mau Mau films made in the 1950s onwards (*Something of Value*, 1957; *Simba*, 1955; *Safari*, 1956), Kenya has commonly served as a cinematographically pleasing, but culturally challenging, backdrop to the melodrama of European life in the former British colony (Anderson 2003).[1] By contrast, Meirelles had come to international attention for co-directing with Kátia Lund the acclaimed *City of God* (2002), a fine-grained portrayal of the lives of the inhabitants of the *favellas* of Rio de Janeiro. If not necessarily an accurate representation of the everyday in Rio de Janeiro, through a tale of gangs, narcotics and the pursuit of an escape from poverty, *The City of God* conveyed something of the reality of life for those living in the slums of the developing world in the age of globalization.

This chapter examines *The Constant Gardener* on three levels. It first considers the specific issue of the conduct in the developing world of trials of pharmaceutical drugs intended for customers in developed countries. The chapter then examines the film's depiction of Kenya. Although the country has not witnessed the sort of controversy surrounding drug trials depicted in the film, it is synonymous with the conditions under which such practices have thrived, namely poverty and corruption. Finally, the chapter considers the film as part of a broader intellectual and cultural attempt to capture the essence of global politics following the end of the Cold War. It positions *The Constant Gardener* alongside an array of non-fiction writing, including some academic, which depicted the world as having entered a period of chaos and endemic instability in the 1990s.

Pharmaceutical Testing in Developing Countries

Le Carré thinks the film is a 'semi-documentary' detailing the activities of multinational pharmaceutical companies in developing countries (Lenzer 2005: 462). It is a subject ripe for exploration in such a fashion given the scale of drug trials in the developing world. Although the exact extent of these trials is not known, figures for individual companies have been publicized. Merck was thought to be conducting half its trials outside of the United States in 2005 and Wyeth over two-thirds (Shah 2005). Angell (2005) believes these figures to be typical for the industry more generally. The attractions to the companies of carrying out such trials in developing countries are obvious. First, the drug companies can escape the rigorous regulatory climate that exists in Europe and North America. Second, such trials can be conducted far more cheaply in developing countries than would be the case elsewhere. Third, public reluctance to participate in such trials in the United States and Europe can be overcome (Shah 2005). Finally, the prior exposure to a wide array of medicines typical of Western European or North American trial subjects can complicate the outcome of the trials of new drugs is not a problem in countries with limited public healthcare (Flaherty, Nelson and Stephens 2000).

Some critics of *The Constant Gardener* try to correct the film's condemnation of the pharmaceutical industry by emphasizing the mutually beneficial nature of the relationship between drug companies and developing countries. Individual drug companies made significant philanthropic gestures towards the developing world. Merck (a U.S.-based company), for example, gained considerable attention in the 1980s after its decision to distribute a treatment for river blindness for free. More recently, Novartis and Aventis subsidized medication for malaria and sleeping sickness (see Miles, Munilla and Covin 2002: 291). To critics, this philanthropy cannot compensate for the unacceptable levels of risk that it is claimed face human subjects of drug trials in developing countries.

All testing of pharmaceutical drugs for commercial purposes is fraught with ethical challenges. Such trials have to carefully balance the ethics of science – the need to carefully control the conditions under which experiments are conducted so as to ensure robust results by using control groups and placebos – and the ethics of medicine – the requirement to provide the best possible care for subjects at all times and thus provide sick trial subjects with the best available treatment. When such trials are conducted by a private company that dilemma is exacerbated by the legal and ethical requirement of such companies to act in the best interests of shareholders (see Drews 2005). Critics of the conduct of pharmaceutical trials in developing countries stress that these dilemmas are exacerbated further in developing countries because of prevailing economic, social, cultural and political conditions.

Those who support an overhaul of the ethical conduct of the pharmaceutical industry find the film particularly powerful. Anthony Robbins (2006: 212), writing in the *Journal of Public Health Policy*, congratulates the makers of *The Constant Gardener*: 'for with this one production that will be seen by millions of people around the world, they will have done more to present the pharmaceutical industry's obstacles to improving health in developing countries than we at *JPHP* can with one hundred articles or that all health and science journals can in a year'. Oxfam (2005) promoted the film as part of its Make Trade Fair campaign and its efforts to persuade Novartis to drop a lawsuit against the Indian government for the latter's production of generic drugs. But it was precisely because Oxfam had to rely upon a fictionalized account of the practices of drug companies in order to create a sense of outrage that otherwise sympathetic campaigners find fault in the film. Even critics of the practices of the pharmaceutical companies drew attention to *The Constant Gardener*'s two principal, implausible premises: first, the fiction that that the behaviour of KDH, Three Bees and the British government was so outrageous that the exposure of them meant death for the Quayles and Bluhm; and, second, that the British press would be astonished by the cover-up (Angell 2005).

Nevertheless, the events depicted in *The Constant Gardener* do not belong solely to the realm of fiction. Corruption and dubious ethical practices related to multinational pharmaceutical companies generally is hardly an implausible subject.[2] More specifically, an example from West Africa bears some resemblance to the scandal depicted in the film. In April 1996 Nigeria's Kano state was in the midst of a meningitis epidemic. The outbreak, together with concurrent high incidences of measles and cholera, claimed the lives of more than 3,000 people. In this context, Pfizer began tests in Kano of an antibiotic, Trovan, intended to counter meningitis more effectively than the then standard treatment, Rocephin. Two hundred children participated in the trial; of which Pfizer acknowledges eleven died. The Nigerian authorities claim the figure is closer to fifty and that nearly two hundred more suffered from other side effects such as loss of hearing and sight and neurological damage.[3] Trovan has subsequently been withdrawn from paediatric use in the United States and the European Union after the discovery that the drug could cause significant liver damage (Lawsuit – Pfizer Fights Back 2007).[4]

The Kano case only came to light as part of investigations by the *Washington Post* in December 2000. The Nigerian drug trial was but one part of a global testing of Trovan by Pfizer that included 13,000 subjects in twenty-seven countries. As the *Washington Post* investigation made clear, it was the Nigerian episode that was the most controversial part of the Trovan trials. After examining the paperwork produced by the global trials prior to approving the drug for use in the United States, FDA inspectors uncovered a series of significant problems with the documentation from the Kano trial. While the FDA has not expanded on the reasons for its decision, Trovan was not approved for use in the United States in paediatric care or in epidemic situations. Pfizer withdrew its application for Trovan to be used in cases of epidemic meningitis prior to the FDA's decision (Stephens 2000). Following the *Washington Post* investigation both the Kano state authorities and the Nigerian Federal Government launched legal action against Pfizer, alleging that the company had not applied for adequate clearance for its trial or gained the consent of its participants. The various parties agreed out of court settlements in 2009 and Pfizer paid over U.S.$75 million into a compensation fund in Kano.[5]

Corruption, Health and Agency in Kenya

Although public health scandals of the sort and scale witnessed in Kano have not been experienced in Kenya, the setting for *The Constant Gardener* is not incidental. Indeed, the film depends upon its location for much of its plausibility. With the none too subtle but mistaken suggestions of Tessa Quayle's sexual impropriety and the subsequent ill-fated police investigations, British and Kenyan audiences of *The Constant Gardener* would have had little difficulty in drawing parallels between her fictional murder and the actual death of Julie Ward, murdered in the Masai Mara national park in 1988. The subsequent long-running investigation has produced numerous theories about why she was killed but no convictions. This process has been extensively covered in the British and Kenyan media, not least due to the efforts of Ward's father to bring his daughter's killers to justice (see Musila 2008; Ward 1991). More significantly, however, *The Constant Gardener*'s plausibility rests on Kenya's synonymy in European and American eyes with poverty – and thus the inaccessibility of medical care – and, most importantly, corruption.

In the film, the ability of Three Bees and KDH to escape prosecution for their illegal activities relies on trial subjects being unwilling to jeopardize their access to continuing medical care, even after the death of family members involved in the trial. This Faustian pact becomes more understandable once the difficulties many Kenyans face in accessing medical care are appreciated. Including both private and public expenditure, per capita spending on healthcare was thought to be U.S.$36 in 2012. By way of contrast, researchers in 2009 estimated that the minimum expenditure per head of population necessary to provide and improve essential healthcare services in the developing world was U.S.$44.[6] Data from the year of the film's release provide further explanation for the hardships participants in the fictional trials were willing to endure in return for free healthcare. In 2005 just 30 per cent of Kenyans in rural areas were living within four kilometres of a health facility. Even in urban areas, only 70 per cent lived within that distance. For those that could make such a journey, the costs of treatment could prove prohibitive and remain so; patients were typically expected to contribute just over half of the total cost of healthcare. Facilities managed or supported by non-governmental organizations where costs for patients are heavily subsidised accounted for just 2 per cent of healthcare expenditure (Export Processing Zones Authority 2005). High quality medical care is thus beyond the means of the majority of Kenyans. Even when Kenyan patients can afford treatment and have access to facilities, the provision of effective care through pharmaceuticals is hindered by significant problems related to the supply and conservation of drugs as well as education on the part of patients (Kenyan Ministry of Health 2003). In such a setting, the attractions of access to well-funded and extensive medical care provided to subjects as part of a pharmaceutical trial are obvious.

The structural impediments to the provision of adequate healthcare caused by Kenya's relative poverty – the country was ranked 143 out of 177 in the United Nations Development Programme's most recent Human Development Index[7] – has, *The Constant Gardener* implies, been exacerbated by endemic corruption by politicians and other public figures. The country's health sector has a far from unblemished record with regards to corruption. Respondents to the Kenyan chapter of Transparency International's annual survey of corruption identified both public hospitals and the

Ministry of Health as being amongst the most frequent demanders of bribes (Transparency International 2009: 16–17). By the time of *The Constant Gardener*'s release in 2005, the extent of corruption within Kenyan public life had become a familiar subject to audiences in Europe and North America. International coverage of the electoral defeat of the Kenya African National Union (KANU) in the December 2002 general election suggested that the endemic corruption since independence in 1963 would end. KANU had been mired in corruption since the presidency of Jomo Kenyatta, the head of state between independence and his death in 1978. The situation worsened under Kenyatta's successor, Daniel arap Moi, particularly following the return to multiparty elections in 1992 after a hiatus of twenty-three years. As incomes fell, the economy collapsed and poverty rose through the 1990s, corruption becoming a vital instrument of control for Moi (Branch 2011). Besides boosting the bank balances of the politicians involved in a series of enormous corruption scandals, the monies accrued allowed for the distribution of funds to retain the support of key allies and the funding of election campaigns as part of a wider informalization of political behaviour (see Branch and Cheeseman 2009).

Any hopes that the situation would improve under Moi's successor, Mwai Kibaki, and his National Rainbow Coalition (NARC) government were short-lived. Following his election victory in 2002 the electorate expected Kibaki's new government to address corruption as a matter of urgency. While some reforms – most notably of the judiciary – were undertaken, the new NARC government demonstrated no great enthusiasm for significant investigations into the financial crimes of the Moi era (Wolf 2006). Furthermore, Kibaki's government itself became mired in corruption. Beginning in April 2004, it became public knowledge that leading figures within NARC had themselves been guilty of gross corruption since taking office a little over a year earlier. The reluctance of the government to investigate this scandal and other such incidents led to the resignation, in February 2005, of John Githongo, the permanent Secretary for Governance and Ethics in the Office of the President. Fearing for his life, Githongo immediately went into exile in Britain, where he remained until his return to Kenya in 2008. Once in Britain, Githongo compiled a dossier of cases of corruption involving senior members of the Kibaki government which he had been prevented from fully investigating (see Wrong 2009).

While *The Constant Gardener* ignores the instrumentality of corruption that Githongo (2006) stresses, where he and the film do agree is in the latter's depiction of the central role played by international capital within Kenyan corruption. Without foreign funds, corrupt practices would at least be reduced in scale. But where the film is significantly at fault is in its ignoring of the role played by figures such as Githongo. While *The Constant Gardener* explores 'the uneasy, divided conscience of the liberal West' torn by the contradictions of capitalism (Scott 2005), it is not a film about Kenya. Kenyan agency is largely ignored by the film.

More is the pity. Long used to the inequities of the global economy, lack of public funds and the dereliction of duty on the part of their political leaders, Kenya's citizens are well accustomed to using their own ingenuity and precious resources in order to shape their daily lives, albeit imperfectly. In the post-colonial period Kenyatta appropriated this enthusiasm for self-help and urged Kenyans to provide for themselves the public services his government thought itself unable to provide (Holmquist 1984). Countless other such examples exist. Of direct relevance to the subject of *The Constant Gardener* one could turn to the myriad of networks within which individuals, households and communities have historically shifted resources to allow members to see out crises (Bollig 1998). Moreover, significant numbers of institutions perform the roles which are only portrayed in *The Constant Gardener* as the 'white woman's burden' of Tessa Quayle.

One such organization is the Mission for Essential Drugs and Supplies (MEDS). Founded in 1986, MEDS is an umbrella body that encompasses the medical facilities managed by the Protestant Christian Health Association of Kenya and the Catholic Kenya Episcopal Conference. MEDS is primarily concerned with the purchasing, supply and administering of affordable and effective pharmaceutical drugs and other medical goods.[8] Initially supported by donor funds, MEDS is now largely sustained by its own revenues and grants from its parent bodies. The group has proved particularly successful in its provision of generic, HIV/AIDS anti-retroviral (ARV) drugs. MEDS played a considerable part in the successful lobbying efforts of 2001 aimed at changing the law to allow Kenyan patients access to such generic drugs. Following that decision MEDS has been at the forefront of the provision of affordable ARV treatments to sufferers of HIV/AIDS in Kenya. MEDS is, in the eyes of the World Health Organization, a model institution providing mass access to high quality and affordable pharmaceutical products in a carefully monitored and safe environment (World Health Organization 2004). As the example of MEDS suggests, Kenyans are well capable, given the opportunities to do so, of coping with whatever challenges their position of relative weakness within the global economy and international relations may produce.

The Coming Anarchy

It is, however, churlish to be too critical of either le Carré's novel or its adaptation for its depiction of either the pharmaceutical industry or its depiction of Kenya. Neither the book nor the film was intended to be narrow expositions of just the ills of Kenyan politics or the pharmaceutical industry. Both the setting and the immediate matters in hand were instead devices through which much bigger questions about the post-Cold War world could be explored. 'For the blink of a star, back there in the early nineties', le Carré (2001b) later wrote, 'something wonderful might have happened: a Marshall Plan, a generous reconciliation of old enemies, a remaking of alliances and, for the Third and Fourth Worlds, a commitment to take on the world's real enemies: starvation, plague, poverty, ecological devastation, despotism and colonialism by all its other names'. As multiparty elections and economic liberalization took hold of the developing world, the triumph of neoliberalism seemed imminent (see Fukuyama 1992). The hopes of le Carré and others, however, quickly collapsed.

Rather than the global peace and prosperity promised by President George Bush (1990), the New World Order quickly turned into something of a nightmare. Democratization was blamed for inciting the civil wars and ethnic violence considered symptomatic of a period in which terms such as 'ethnic cleansing' and 'genocide' became the stuff of international relations and local politics across the globe (see Chua 2002). Hobsbawm observes 'the decline in the acceptance of state legitimacy, of the voluntary acceptance of obligation to ruling authorities and their laws by those who live on their territories, whether as citizens or as subjects' (2008: 36–7). State disintegration enabled radical changes to the economic sphere. According to Eric Hobsbawm, the willingness of private capital to be subject to the state's fiat declined: 'We have a rapidly globalising global world economy based on transnational private firms that are doing their best to live outside the range of state law and taxes, which severely limits the ability of even big governments to control their national economies' (2008: 36–7). The deregulation and the systematic removal of barriers to the international movement of capital both formed significant parts of the neoliberal reforms undertaken across the developing world under structural adjustment programmes. As a consequence, critics such as Naomi Klein (2008) argue that the exploitative grasp of international capitalism enclosed the everyday lives of a great many more people across the globe.

The actual costs and benefits of globalization for developing countries are (of course) much debated. What cannot be questioned, however, is the extent to which the expansion of global labour, capital and commodity markets has been widely perceived to have weakened the control of national governments over the activities of multinational corporations. In a context of environmental degradation and the HIV/AIDS pandemic, the removal of barriers to international capitalism and the removal of ideology from global and local political debates led to Robert Kaplan's controversial *The Coming Anarchy* (2001; see Hoffman, this volume). In the book and in the articles that preceded it (Kaplan 1994a, 1994b), Kaplan depicts the developing world as a place where greed is unchecked by ideology and insecurity is rampant. Politics and criminality are, according to Kaplan, becoming one and the same thing in sub-Saharan Africa and elsewhere as the well-being of the world's population is sacrificed in struggles for increasingly scarce natural resources and commodities.

This dubious depiction of an utterly chaotic and anarchic world has not, of course, been accepted uncritically by academics. In relation to sub-Saharan Africa, a significant body of scholarship has attempted to explore the underlying reasons for the political insecurity and economic uncertainty that has characterized the historical path of many African states since the early 1990s.[9] Despite such efforts, it is the anarchic paradigm of Kaplan et al. that finds expression in *The Constant Gardener*. As private corporate interests appeared to supplant strategic, national concerns as the foundation of international relations, it seemed to le Carré (2001b: 11) that:

> [W]e look on apparently helpless while rainforests are wrecked to the tune of millions of square miles every year, native agricultural communities are systematically deprived of their livelihoods, uprooted and made homeless, protestors are hanged and shot, the loveliest corners of the world are invaded and desecrated, and tropical paradises are turned into rotting wastelands with sprawling, disease-ridden megacities at their center.

The book le Carré then produced and the subsequent adaptation were thus an explicit attempt 'to illustrate this argument'. He would agree a great deal with several of the writers discussed above. At the heart of the world's troubles in the 1990s, le Carré identified the collapse of national sovereignty and the growing influence of the private sector on domestic policy and foreign relations. Nation states had, he argued, become 'the hired mouthpieces of multibillion-dollar multinational corporations that view the exploitation of the world's sick and dying as a sacred duty to their shareholders' (2001b: 13). Le Carré found in the activities of pharmaceutical multinationals 'the most eloquent example' of the 'crimes of unbridled capitalism' that he thought epitomised the post-Cold-War age. 'Big Pharma, as it is

83

known,' le Carré wrote (ibid.: 12), 'offered everything: the hopes and dreams we have of it; its vast, partly realized potential for good; and its pitch-dark underside, sustained by huge wealth, pathological secrecy, corruption and greed'. For le Carré, the pharmaceutical industry was a metaphor for the hopes and attendant disappointments of the New World Order.

But, viewed from Kenya, what was new about this New World Order? The notion of the Kenyan state as having previously protected its subjects and citizens has little historical precedence. In common with other African colonies, the Kenyan colonial state established at the end of the nineteenth century was dedicated to what Crawford Young (1994: 2) terms 'the vocation of domination'. In particular, the Kenyan colonial state used domination to protect the interests of its small population of European settlers rather than its African majority (Berman 1992; Berman and Lonsdale 1992). Although imbued with unprecedented legitimacy by independence, the use of corruption, violence and ethnicity as part of the toolkit of governance meant that the post-colonial state soon suffered from a similar crisis of legitimacy as its colonial predecessor. Structural adjustment reforms in the 1980s and 1990s further certainly reduced the state's capacity to protect its citizens from the adverse effects of global market forces, but its rulers had not previously been much concerned by such matters (Branch 2011).

As this brief survey of Kenyan history suggests, the parlous condition of the state that *The Constant Gardener* depicts is much older than the film's makers may think. Similarly, the imbalance in power between Western capital and African societies that the film illustrates is hardly new either (Bayart 2000). *The Constant Gardener* sets out to capture the *zeitgeist* of the post-Cold War world and convey a sense of crisis and a new historical era. But what it actually depicts is just the latest episode in much deeper historical processes of state-building and capitalism. Furthermore, the film demonstrates the limited range of modest possible responses to these processes when socialism is discredited so widely. Instead of meaningful debate about what le Carré terms 'rogue capitalism', the film leaves us with two possible but limited courses of action. The first is the worthy but limited gesture of humanitarianism, represented in the film by Tessa Quayle, herself based on Yvette Pierpaoli, a French aid worker. The second is the advocacy of single-issue non-governmental organisations, as depicted by the film's pharmaceutical watchdog, Hippo, which is based on the Germany-based BUKO Pharma-Kampagne.[10] To the cast and crew's credit, the Constant Gardener Trust was established after the film's completion to support health and education projects in Kenya.[11] Such individuals and organisations play important roles in softening the edges of global capitalism, but hardly provide the basis for a sustained critique of the wide range of economic, political and challenges posed by the market to countries like Kenya in the post-Cold War era. As Tony Judt writes, 'we seem unable to conceive of alternatives' (2011: 2).

Conclusion

As a film about Kenya and Kenyans *The Constant Gardener* resorts to type. Despite Meirelles' pedigree, *The Constant Gardener* bears more than a passing resemblance to Sydney Pollack's *Out of Africa* (1985). In terms of cinematography, both films make much of the contrast between northern Europe and eastern Africa. *Out of Africa*'s Denmark and *The Constant Gardener*'s Britain and Germany are both 'washed out' and grey. Kenya by contrast – at least outside of Nairobi in the case of *The Constant Gardener* – is brightly lit, indeed dazzling in the opening scene of Meirelles' film. The resemblances between the Danish Karen Blixen, the central character in *Out of Africa*, and the British Tessa Quayle are startling. Both find themselves on the margins of the social circle that came with their choice of husband and dedicate themselves to the welfare of the Kenyans they come into contact with as part of their attempt to escape their social lives. But in both films those Kenyans are portrayed mainly as the victims of exploitation.

The Constant Gardener's intellectual significance is twofold. First, it is a searing critique of the testing of pharmaceutical products in developing countries that forms part of a much larger body of work produced in the main by investigative journalists and medical practitioners. One does not have to agree with the particular characterization of the pharmaceutical industry in *The Constant Gardener* to agree that by increasing awareness of ethical and legal issues related to drug trials in developing countries, the film has contributed towards a move towards greater public awareness of potential risks and the tighter regulation of the practice. Most importantly, the film is an invaluable cultural artefact of a particular historical moment in the aftermath of the Cold War during which it appeared that the twin forces of globalization were spreading exploitation and insecurity across the developing world.

Notes

1. See also *Out of Africa* (dir. Sydney Pollack, 1985), *White Mischief* (dir. Michael Radford, 1988) and *I Dreamed of Africa* (dir. Hugh Hudson, 2000).
2. See, for example, discussions of the controversy surrounding the approval given in 2004 for Merck's Vioxx and the behaviour of the Italian and European-wide regulator, Duilio Poggiolini, in 1993 (see Law 2006: 20, 87–94).
3. See 'Q&A: Nigeria Sues Pfizer', published on the BBC News website, 5 June 2007. Retrieved 15 March 2009 from http://news.bbc.co.uk/1/hi/world/africa/6721771.stm
4. See 'Nigeria: Lawsuit – Pfizer Fights Back' in *This Day*, 6 June 2007. Retrieved 15 March 2009 from http://allafrica.com/stories/200706060108.html
5. See 'Pfizer Settles Remaining Nigeria, U.S. Trovan Suits', published on the Reuters website, 23 February 2010. Retrieved 14 November 2012 from http://www.reuters.com/article/2011/02/23/us-pfizer-idUSTRE71M18U20110223
6. See World Health Organisation (2012) and Xu et al (2010).
7. See 'Kenya Country Profile: Human Development Indictors', published on United Nations Development Programme website. Retrieved 14 November 2012 from http://hdrstats.undp.org/en/countries/profiles/ken:html
8. The Mission for Essential Drugs and Supplies website can be found at http://www.meds.or.ke/
9. See, for a wide array of opinions on such questions: Bates (2008), Bayart,

Ellis and Hibou (1999), Cooper (2002), Mbembe (2001) and Young (2004).
10. The Buko Pharma-Kampagne website can be found at http://www.bukopharma.de/english/
11. The Constant Gardener Trust website can be found at http://www.constantgardenertrust.org/

Filmography

Brooks, R. (Dir.) 1957. *Something of Value* (Metro-Goldwyn-Mayer).
Hudson, H. (Dir.) 2000. *I Dreamed of Africa* (Columbia Pictures Corporation, De Wolfe Music, Jaffilms).
Hurst, B.D. (Dir.) 1955. *Simba* (Group Film Productions Limited).
Meirelles, F. (Dir.) 2002. *City of God* (O2 Filmes, VideoFilmes, Globo Filmes, Lumiere, Wild Bunch, Hank Levine Film).
———. (Dir.) 2005. *The Constant Gardener* (Focus Features, U.K. Film Council, Potboiler Productions, Scion Films).
Pollack, S. (Dir.) 1985. *Out of Africa* (Mirage Enterprises, Universal Pictures).
Radford, M. (Dir.) 1987. *White Mischief* (Goldcrest Films International, Nelson Entertainment, Power Tower Investments, Umbrella Films).
Young, T. (Dir.) 1956. *Safari* (Warwick Film Productions).

References

Anderson, D. 2003. 'Mau Mau at the Movies: Contemporary Representations of an Anti-Colonial War', *South African Historical Journal* 48(1): 71–89.
Angell, M. 2005. 'The Body Hunters', *New York Review of Books*, 6 October.
Bates, R. 2008. *When Things Fall Apart: State Failure in Late-Century Africa*. Cambridge: Cambridge University Press.
Bayart, J.-F. 2000. 'Africa in the World: A History of Extraversion', *African Affairs*, 99 (395): 217–67.
Bayart, J.-F., S. Ellis and B. Hibou. 1999. *The Criminalization of the State in Africa*. Oxford: James Currey.
Berman, B. 1992. *Control and Crisis in Colonial Kenya: The Dialectic of Domination*. London: James Currey.
Berman, B. and J. Lonsdale. 1992. *Unhappy Valley: Conflict in Kenya and Africa*. London: James Currey.
Bollig, M. 1998. 'Moral Economy and Self-Interest: Kinship, Friendship, and Exchange Among the Pokot (N.W. Kenya)', in T. Schweizer and D. White (eds), *Kinship, Networks, and Exchange*. Cambridge: Cambridge University Press, pp. 137–57.

Branch, D. 2011. *Kenya: Between Hope and Despair, 1963–2011*. New Haven & London: Yale University Press.
Branch, D. and N. Cheeseman. 2009. 'Democratization, Sequencing, and State Failure in Africa: Lessons from Kenya', *African Affairs* 108(430): 1–26.
Bush, G. 1990. 'Address before a Joint Session of the Congress on the Persian Gulf Crisis and the Budget Deficit', 11 September, *George Bush Presidential Library and Museum*. Retrieved 2 March 2009 from http://bushlibrary. tamu.edu/research/public_papers.php?id=2217&year=1990&month=9
Carré, J. le. 2001a. *The Constant Gardener*. London: Hodder & Stoughton.
_____. 2001b. 'In Place of Nations', *The Nation*, 9 April 2001, 11.
_____. 2011. *The Secret Pilgrim*. London: Penguin.
Chua, A. 2002. *World on Fire: How Exporting Free Market Democracy Breeds Ethnic Hatred and Global Instability*. New York: Doubleday.
Cooper, F. 2002. *Africa since 1940: The Past of the Present*. Cambridge: Cambridge University Press.
DeYoung, K. and D. Nelson. 2000. 'Latin America is Ripe for Trials, and Fraud: Frantic Pace Could Overwhelm Controls', *Washington Post*, 21 December, A01.
Drews, J. 2005. 'Drug Research: Between Ethical Demands and Economic Constraints', in M. Santoro and T. Gorrie (eds), *Ethics and the Pharmaceutical Industry*. Cambridge: Cambridge University Press, pp. 21–36.
Export Processing Zones Authority. 2005. *Kenya's Pharmaceutical Industry 2005*. Nairobi: Republic of Kenya.
Flaherty, M.P. and D. Struck. 2000. 'Life by Luck of the Draw: In Third World Drug Tests, Some Subjects Go Untreated', *Washington Post*, 22 December, A01.
Flaherty, M.P., D. Nelson and J. Stephens, 2000. 'Testing Tidal Wave Hits Overseas: On Distant Shores, Drug Firms Avoid Delays – and Scrutiny', *Washington Post*, 18 December.
Fukuyama, F. 1992. *The End of History and the Last Man*. London: Hamish Hamilton.
Githongo, J. 2006. 'Inequality, Ethnicity and the Fight Against Corruption in Africa: A Kenyan Perspective', *Economic Affairs* 26(4): 19–23.
Gussow, M. 2000. 'In a Plot Far From the Cold, Le Carre Sums Up the Past', *New York Times* website, 19 December 2000. Retried 8 November 2012 from http://www.nytimes.com/2000/12/19/books/in-a-plot-far-from-the-cold-le-carre-sums-up-the-past.html?pagewanted=1
Hobsbawm, E. 2008. *Globalisation, Democracy and Terrorism*. London: Abacus.
Holmquist, F. 1984. 'Self-Help: The State and Peasant Leverage in Kenya', *Africa* 53(3): 72–91.

Judt, T. 2011. *Ill Fares the Land: A Treatise on Our Present Discontents*. London: Penguin.
Kaplan, R. 2001. *The Coming Anarchy: Shattering the Dreams of the Post Cold War*. New York: Vintage.
Kaplan, R.D. 1994a. 'The Coming Anarchy: how scarcity, crime, overpopulation and disease are rapidly destroying the social fabric of our planet', *Atlantic Monthly*, February.
———. 1994b. 'Into the bloody new world: a moral pragmatism for America in an age of mini-holocausts', *Washington Post*, 17 April 1994.
Kenyan Ministry of Health. 2003. *Assessment of the Pharmaceutical Situation in Kenya: A Baseline Survey 2003*. Nairobi: Republic of Kenya.
Klein, N. 2008. *The Shock Doctrine: The Rise of Disaster Capitalism*. London: Penguin.
LaFraniere, S., M.P. Flaherty and J. Stephens. 2000. 'The Dilemma: Submit or Suffer; "Uniformed Consent" is Rising Ethic of the Drug Test Boom', *Washington Post*, 19 December, A01.
Law, J. 2006. *Big Pharma: How the World's Biggest Drug Companies Control Illness*. London: Constable.
Lenzer, J. 2005. 'The Constant Gardener', *British Medical Journal*, 331(7514): 462.
Mbembe, A. 2001. *On the Postcolony*. Berkeley: University of California Press.
Miles, M., L. Munilla and J. Covin. 2002. '*The Constant Gardener* Revisited: The Effect of Social Blackmail on the Marketing Concept, Innovation and Entrepreneurship', *Journal of Business Ethics* 41(3): 287–295.
Musila, G. 2008. 'Inscribing the Memories on Dead Bodies: Sex, Gender, and State Power in the Julie Ward Death in Kenya', *Journal of Eastern African Studies* 2(3): 439–455.
Oxfam. 2005. 'On Location in Kibera', Make Trade Fair Campaign. Retrieved 13 March 2009 from http://www.maketradefair.com/en/index.php?file=constant05.htm
Robbins, A. 2006. 'Film Review: The Constant Gardener', *Journal of Public Health Policy* 27(2006): 211–212.
Scott, A.O. 2005. 'Digging Up the Truth in a Heart of Darkness', *New York Times*, 31 August.
Shah, S. 2005. '"The Constant Gardener": What the Movie Missed', *The Nation*, 30 August.
Stephens, J. 2000. 'Where Profits and Lives Hang in Balance; Finding an Abundance of Subjects and Lack of Oversight Abroad, Big Drugs Companies Test Offshore to Speed Products to Market', *Washington Post*, 17 December, A01.
Transparency International – Kenya. 2009. *The Kenya Bribery Index 2008*. Nairobi. Transparency International – Kenya. Retrieved 14 November

2012 from http://www.tikenya.org/index.php?option=com_content&view=article&id=72&Itemid=66#
Ward, J. 1991. *The Animals are Innocent: The Search for Julie's Killers*. London: Headline.
Wolf, T. 2006. 'Immunity or Accountability? Daniel Toroitich arap Moi: Kenya's First Retired President', in R. Southall and H. Melber (eds), *Legacies of Power: Leadership Change and Former Presidents in African Politics*. Cape Town: HSRC, pp. 197–232.
World Health Organization. 2004. *Mission for Essential Drugs and Supplies, Kenya: Case Study*. Geneva: World Health Organization.
———. 2012. *World Health Statistics 2012*. Geneva: World Health Organization.
Wrong, M. 2009. *It's Our Turn to Eat: The Story of a Kenyan Whistle Blower*. London: Fourth Estate.
Xu, K., P. Saksena, M. Jowett, C. Indikadahena, J. Kutzin and D. Evans. 2010. 'Exploring the Thresholds of Health Expenditure for Protection Against Financial Risk'. World Health Report (2010) Background Paper 19. Geneva: World Health Organization.
Young, C. 1994. *The African Colonial State in Comparative Perspective*. New Haven & London: Yale University Press.
———. 2004. 'The End of the Post-Colonial State in Africa? Reflections on Changing African Political Dynamics', *African Affairs* 103(410): 23–49.

Four

War in the City, Crime in the Country
Blood Diamond and the Representation of Violence in the Sierra Leone War

Danny Hoffman

The final shots of Freetown, capital of Sierra Leone, come in the forty-eighth minute of Edward Zwick's 2006 film *Blood Diamond*. What had until that point been an unstated but pronounced tension between the rural and the urban in Sierra Leone gives way to a more conventional Hollywood narrative of Africa. For the remaining ninety minutes West Africa is jungle, river, farm and sky. African fighters are bush warriors, a natural feature of the rainforest and savannah. The only urban settings are global cities such as London, Mumbai, Antwerp and Cape Town. What happens in the African bush is implicitly linked to these metropoles, but urban West Africa is erased from both the film's unfolding transnational drama of violence and trade, and its personal drama of redemption and justice.

Those final scenes of Freetown are, however, illustrative. They make visible a set of common global fantasies of African urban space and of contemporary African warfare. In the director's own words, these fast-paced, violent, disorienting scenes 'show in an almost *Clockwork Orange* way what was happening in those places when everything had gone as wrong as it possibly could'.[1] Both Zwick's cinematic reference and the description of Freetown as a place in which everything has gone 'wrong' point toward a way of framing both African conflict and the African city as Hollywood apocalypse. In this archetypical city violence is represented as an end in itself. It is not intended to achieve anything beyond its own performance. It is irrational violence, predetermined by the nature of the continent and by the savagery endemic to urban Africa.

This stands in marked contrast to the tenor of the opening scenes of the film. The violence that we see depicted in the countryside of Sierra Leone is no less traumatic or graphic. But it is not anarchic. The film implies that when violence comes to the villages of Sierra Leone it is methodical, calculated, and criminal. Violence there is utilitarian. It has a logic. Its goals might be reprehensible and illegitimate, but its performance is rational. Its Hollywood references are less *Clockwork Orange* than *The Godfather*.

In what follows I trace *Blood Diamond*'s contrasting depictions of violence in urban space and its depiction of violence in Sierra Leone's up-country provinces. Each relies on a globally circulating caricature of African war. But it is important to note that it is not the same caricature. *Blood Diamond*'s depiction of conflict in the city repeats the now familiar fantasy of a continent that, in the wake of the Cold War, has reverted to a primitive state of pure violence (see Branch, this volume). Yet what *Blood Diamond* makes clear is that this fantasy, now two decades old, remains a primarily urban fantasy. The Africa of *Blood Diamond* is not, as *The Economist* famously put it, 'Hopeless Africa'.[2] The narrative is more specific than that: in *Blood Diamond* (and beyond), the African city has become the 'hopeless city'.

The war in Sierra Leone's rural areas is represented by the more recent fantasy of pure criminality. As the trade in natural resources has become more visible in the world press, and as the U.S. and

European security sectors have become more obsessed with Africa's so-called 'ungoverned' spaces, conflict in rural space is cast as a problem of law. Typified by the opening scenes in *Blood Diamond*, violence in rural Africa is not primordial; it is simply illegitimate and illegal.

Each of these narratives is depoliticized. The evolution of the post-Cold War 'primordialism' narrative of African warfare into an urban narrative, and the rise of the criminal narrative of African violence (largely as a consequence of the U.S.A.'s Global War on Terror) have not made African politics any more legible on the world stage. When it was released, in 2006, *Blood Diamond* was cast as a political film for its critique of the trade in stones from conflict zones. But the twin cinematic lenses through which *Blood Diamond* renders that conflict visible (the 'hopeless city' versus the 'criminal rural') do little to address the complex politics that tied the city to the country and gave meaning to Sierra Leone's long and tragic war.

Blood Diamond and the War in Sierra Leone

When *Blood Diamond* was released, in 2006, the war in Sierra Leone had 'officially' been over for four years. It began a decade and a half earlier when the Revolutionary United Front (RUF) crossed the border from Liberia and launched its first attacks in the eastern Kailahun District. The small RUF insurgency quickly lost public support. Its self-description as a popular liberation army grew increasingly implausible as it targeted civilians and preyed on rural communities throughout the east. In contrast to the classic models of rural popular insurgency, the RUF sustained itself by sacking villages and trafficking diamonds mined in the rich alluvial fields of Kono. Charles Taylor, the rebel leader turned President of neighbouring Liberia, traded cash and weapons for many of these stones. So, too, did a range of actors from Lebanese businessmen to the Sierra Leone Army.[3] The RUF bolstered its ranks by forcing civilians to serve as combatants and camp followers, and by deploying mercenaries from other parts of West Africa and, occasionally, beyond.

Blood Diamond purports to pick up the story of the Sierra Leone war in 1999. In reality the RUF had by this point already joined with a mutinous faction of the state army and ruled Sierra Leone through military junta for some ten months. Driven from the capital in February 1998, the RUF/AFRC 'People's Army'[4] gathered strength in the countryside and on 6 January 1999 launched a devastating attack on Freetown (an attack that is restaged in the film). Although the invasion did not topple the government a second time, it did massive damage to the city. For the next three years the RUF continued a low intensity conflict in the countryside against an array of pro-government militias, West African and United Nations peacekeepers and British paratroopers. Control of the diamond mines was a recurrent issue. The various factions clashed militarily in and around Kono, and at one point a perverse ceasefire agreement gave RUF leader Foday Sankoh control of the Sierra Leone government's Ministry of Mines. As the war in Sierra Leone finally drew to a close, many of the RUF's more seasoned fighters slipped across the border to join the escalating conflict in Liberia.

The opening title sequence of *Blood Diamond* broadly locates the film in this timeline (though it offers little detail) and provides a pithy summation of the film's politics:

> Sierra Leone 1999 / Civil war rages for control of the diamond fields. / Thousands have died and millions have become refugees. / None of whom has ever seen a diamond.

The plot begins in a coastal Mende village.[5] Fisherman Solomon Vandy (Djimon Honsou) is separated from his family when the RUF attacks. Vandy is captured and forced to mine diamonds in Kono, unaware that his wife and daughters escaped to the refugee camps of Guinea and that his son, Dia (Kagiso Kuypers), has been abducted by the RUF.

Vandy's story goes from typical Sierra Leone war story to the film's driving force when he discovers an unusually large gem, which he buries during the chaos of a government attack on the mine. Vandy is taken as a prisoner to Freetown, from which point the film becomes the story of two, intertwined obsessions: Vandy's quest to find his lost son, and a variety of characters' fixation on the buried stone. Chief among these is Danny Archer (Leonardo DiCaprio), a white veteran of the South African Defence Force (SADF) campaigns in Angola who becomes Vandy's heroic counterpart. Archer, through a combination of wile and race-based privilege, offers crucial assistance in locating and rescuing Dia Vandy. Solomon Vandy, in turn, is Archer's key to finding buried treasure. This windfall from recovering the buried diamond is supposed to allow the Rhodesian-born Archer to finally leave Africa for good.[6]

The double quest at the heart of the film is launched by two key moments of violence. The first is the small-scale raid on the Vandy family's village in the opening moments of the film, in which Solomon loses his son to the RUF's Captain Poison (David Harewood) and is pressed into forced labour. The second is the massive Freetown invasion, presumably modelled on the actual attack of 6 January 1999. As the rebels set about destroying the city, Archer dangles before Vandy the prospect that he 'knows people, white people' who can locate Sierra Leoneans displaced by the war. In return for helping him find the buried diamond, Archer will lead Vandy out of the falling city and to his vanished family.

In this chapter I take up these two moments of violence in more detail. I begin, however, by contextualizing them in the urban/rural nexus of Sierra Leone's war – both as it played out on the ground in the 1990s and as it exists in the global imaginary of contemporary African violence.

The Urban/Rural Relationship

Most observers point to the complex relationship between the urban and the rural as crucial to understanding the Sierra Leone war. Like many sub-Saharan African countries, Sierra Leone has one major urban centre: its capital, Freetown. The urban/rural divide is thus both quite stark and closely tied to the particulars of a single metropolitan space. The Krio colloquialism *salone* refers alternately to the capital and to the country of Sierra Leone as a whole, while 'I am going to town' (*A de go towhn* in Krio) can refer to a journey to the capital from anywhere in the country.[7] The capital is both the administrative and financial centre of the nation, and it is home to the majority of the nation's elite. Although there are a handful of population centres spread throughout Sierra Leone, only Freetown has the requisite population density, infrastructure, and cosmopolitan élan to be widely thought of as 'the city'.

Freetown's exceptionalism within Sierra Leone is not absolute, of course. Generations of Freetownians trace their ancestry to up-country villages and maintain a literal or imaginative connection to those communities. Social networks that span the urban/rural divide are important conduits for the flow of capital, goods, information and people. And yet those living in the city were remarkably ignorant of the war's evolution in the countryside. Freetown residents, and indeed the entire Sierra Leonean government, failed to appreciate the extent of the conflict as it moved across the south, east and north of the country. For some time after the news of the RUF invasion reached Freetown, even high-ranking Sierra Leone military personnel referred to the conflict as an extension of provincial political squabbles (see Gberie 2005: 66; Richards 1996: 22).

Whatever the extent of the initial misreading of events beyond the city's borders, as the war progressed Freetown began to figure in the war's evolution in complex ways. Despite its 'bush' origins, the RUF's early leadership was largely composed of students and self-identified revolutionaries from Freetown (Abdullah 2004; Peters 2006; Rashid 2004; Richards 1996). In the mid 1990s the pro-government Civil Defence Forces militia, based in the rural southeast, was viewed by at least some of its Mende nationalist leaders as an opportunity to contest Freetown's elite patronage system (Fithen 1999). The two wartime coups were the result of officers stationed in the countryside feeling dangerously marginalized from the military and government centres of power in the capital (Gberie 2005;

Kandeh 1996; Keen 2005). And more than once during the war the Sierra Leone Army swelled its ranks by recruiting underemployed urban youth for the front lines, a tactic that exacerbated tensions between rural communities and the increasingly undisciplined and predatory military (Reno 1995, 2003).

In contrast to its urban origins, the RUF has been characterized as a movement profoundly shaped by its existence in networks of rural forest enclaves. The fact that so many of the RUF's commanders and foot soldiers lived in relative isolation in the villages and base camps of the countryside seems to have fed a sense of paranoia and narcissism that ultimately translated into extreme violence (Keen 2005; Peters 2006; Richards 1996, 1999). For them urban space and its inhabitants were targets in multiple senses: objects of fantasy and desire to be captured, and sources of fear and loathing to be destroyed. What's more, the RUF, like most fighting factions in this region, saw spectacular and devastating attacks on the city as a way to brand themselves as legitimate and powerful actors before both national and international audiences (see Gberie 2005; Hoffman 2004).

What this amounts to is a sense among scholars that the relationship between city and rural areas constitutes a 'problem' in understanding the trajectory of this war. The recruitment of urban youth to fight in the countryside; the information disconnect of the capital from the country; the prominent place of the rainforest in the cultural imaginary of an urbanizing populace; the role of forest resources like diamonds and timber in financing the war; the extraordinary levels of violence within the city – all suggest that understanding the Sierra Leone war means reckoning with the complex relationship between rural and urban spaces.

The Urban/Rural Dichotomy

Despite its obvious importance, the urban/rural relationship in the Sierra Leone war becomes a stark dichotomy in most press accounts of the war, security policy analyses and fictionalized accounts of the country's violence. The effect is to erase the importance of one of these spaces while at the same time misunderstanding the other.

The city in many of these formulations embodies the inscrutability and intractability of post-Cold-War African conflicts. The most famous account of the war in Sierra Leone remains journalist Robert D. Kaplan's 1994 *Atlantic Monthly* essay 'The Coming Anarchy' (see Branch, this volume). Though often cited as a particularly egregious portrayal of the inscrutability and intractability of post-Cold-War African violence as a whole, it is really the city against which Kaplan sets his analysis. What he describes is in fact an old narrative nightmare of urbanizing Africa: a continent that suffers war and chaos because its people – particularly its male youth – lose their 'natural' social restraints when they move from the village to the city. Based in part on his travels in West Africa, most notably in wartime Sierra Leone, Kaplan argues that rapidly expanding cities in the Global South are by definition threatening. 'In cities in six West African countries,' Kaplan (2000: 5) writes, 'I saw similar young men everywhere – hordes of them. They were like loose molecules in a very unstable social fluid, a fluid that was clearly on the verge of igniting'.

For Kaplan these 'hordes' make the West African city a space of inherent insecurity and warfare (see Introduction and Eltringham, this volume, for a discussion of Africans as a 'frantic mass'). It is a space of violence 'about' nothing, a degenerative form of warfare as symptom of urbanization and culture loss.

Kaplan's poetic construction of African urbanity is echoed through much of the emergent literature on the threat that African cities pose to global security. In the 2003 United States Department of the Army Urban Operations field manual FM 3–06 (2003), cities (especially the cities of the Global South) are portrayed as the real enemy: 'Uncontrolled urban growth,' write the manual's authors, result in 'general instability, competing power structures, disease and pollution,' and that '[i]n many urban stability operations and support operations, these may be the primary "threats" to mission accomplishment' (3–34).

For the Urban Operations manual (3–38), as for Kaplan, the spark that will supposedly ignite the volatile mix of the city is young men:

> Urban areas with a large youth population may also help to generate conditions for instability ... Urbanization and population growth are more dangerous when they combine to produce a cohort of young urban dwellers separated from traditional social controls, such as village elders and clan leaders.

The manual offers no wisdom about the relationship between these two spheres. Its analysis is grounded in a commonsense understanding that the city and the country are divergent worlds: the former a space of degenerate absence; the latter a space of natural social control.

One of the most popular fictional accounts of the war, Uzodinma Iweala's *Beasts of No Nation* (2005), similarly portrays the city as a zone of particular and extreme terrors.[8] The child-soldier protagonist Agu is abducted and conscripted into the rebel forces from his home village. His one encounter with 'town' begins with the story his commander tells of the founding of the city, a legend the moral of which is that 'you can never be trusting anybody or anything in this town' (2005: 100). The city Agu discovers is a rotting place. It is severely damaged by the war, but this destruction comes across as only one element of a more profound disintegration. Though Agu has by this point encountered human death on a mass scale in the bush, he is considerably more revolted by the moral corruption of the urban social environment and by the way the city streets swell with refuse, dead animals, and living people. Agu's stay in the city completes his fall from idyllic village childhood to rebel beast.

In short, violence in the city circulates through each of these narratives as the eruption of senseless, total war, an unavoidable consequence of urbanism itself. By contrast, the prevailing discourse of violence in the countryside is pared down radically to a single element: greed. The fact that the illicit diamond trade played such a central role in the Sierra Leonean war (coupled with an inability or unwillingness to engage with the combatants' conception of their own activities) meant that rural spheres of conflict are most often understood in terms of criminality rather than conflict. In more or less sophisticated commentaries on the war, the rural spaces of Sierra Leone are simply the repositories of natural resource wealth, and the combatants who wage war there are one-dimensional profiteers.

The best known of these interpretations, by economists Paul Collier and Anke Hoeffler (see, for example, Collier 2000; Collier and Hoeffler 2000), attempted to give some complexity to the simplistic equation of 'rebellion' with 'crime'. But it did so by arguing for a more nuanced understanding of the varieties of crime represented by African violence rather than taking seriously the politics of that violence. 'Grievance', according to this framework, is at best an obfuscation of the far more reliable predictors of mass African violence – access to wealth from natural resources.

In its case against the pro-government Civil Defence Force (CDF), the prosecution at the Special Court for Sierra Leone similarly refused to countenance the possibility that the pro-government CDF militia had legitimately taken up arms against the RUF or the People's Army because of *political* grievances.[9] In his opening statement in June 2004 the prosecutor David Crane maintained that the CDF defence of the government could only constitute a joint criminal enterprise:

> The issues before you are not, cannot be, political. We have not charged political crimes ... Politics must remain barred from the proceedings ... We allege that the accused committed international crimes, their actions were criminal acts, their mindset criminal – not political. Now defending one's nation is a just cause ... The just cause of a civil defence force in Sierra Leone, set up to defend a nation became perverted and was twisted beyond measure ... Under their leadership these accused war criminals turned what should have been a just cause into an unjust effect – serious breaches of the laws designed to protect humanity. These so-called defenders of the nation were really offenders of the nation looking out for their own self-interests.[10]

There is a specifically rural imaginary at work in the SCSL prosecutor's insistence that politics had no place in the pro-government militia's activities. Although the case did touch briefly upon CDF activities in Bo and Kenema (the second and third largest towns), it completely erased the CDF's defence of Freetown, and most of the 'Black December' campaign to push CDF fighters toward the capital in 1997. Removing Freetown from the calculus of CDF actions allowed the prosecutor to privilege the group's efforts to claim territory in the country's economic centre (the rural diamond fields), but sidestep their efforts to reclaim the political centre (Freetown).

This myopia of the rural is even more pronounced in the prologue to journalist Greg Campbell's 2002 book on the trade in Sierra Leone's conflict diamonds. Campbell positions the West African landscape and its mineral wealth as key to understanding everything about the war – and Sierra Leone itself. 'It's not difficult to see why Sierra Leone is low on most people's list of places in which to intervene,' he writes. After describing Sierra Leone as a victim of the usual African plagues of corruption and 'thuggish leaders', he adds the following:

> The climate is also horrible: Muggy and humid throughout the year, the tropical landscape is an incubator for malarial mosquitoes, polio, yellow fever, river blindness, and dozens of other deadly diseases. During the rainy season, everything – whether indoors or outdoors – remains wet for five months. During the dry season, harmattan winds from the Sahel and Sahara Deserts sandblast the country and the sunlight seems to be focused by a huge magnifying glass. The raw and unrelenting natural environment is reflected in the people and the actions of some of them in times of war. (Campbell 2002: xxi)

Here the fighters in Sierra Leone's war take on the savage character of their rural environment. Their ruthlessness in pursuing profit from the earth is forged of the same harsh natural processes that formed the gems themselves. The nature of the links between Africanness, masculinity, natural-resource wealth and violence are for the most part unexplored. They seem, in Campbell's book as in so many other treatments of that nexus, to be so obvious that they require no explanation.

As an articulation of a global fantasy of contemporary African warfare, *Blood Diamond* is most interestingly read through the way it contrasts these conceptions of post-Cold-War violence (irrational urban versus criminal rural) early in the film. I turn now to a detailed reading of the two most consequential representations of these modes of violence: the opening RUF attack on the small coastal fishing community in which the Vandys live, and the massive assault on Freetown. Although they are not the only images of violence in the film, they most significantly direct the course of the plot. They are also the scenes designed to carry most of the weight of *Blood Diamond*'s larger commentary about the nature of violence and African war.

Crime in the Country

The opening scenes of *Blood Diamond* depict an idyllic coastal village. Though actually filmed in Mozambique (with Sierra Leonean hill-scapes digitally inserted), the intent is to represent rural Sierra Leone as 'naturally' peaceful. The audience sees a family beginning its day, followed by the intricate, beautifully choreographed labour of net fishermen on the water. As Solomon Vandy and his son Dia walk home in the afternoon, Dia relates his schoolteacher's lesson of the day: Sierra Leone was 'founded as a utopia', and when the war is over it will once again be a paradise. In the director's commentary, Zwick's voice-over in these opening scenes recounts how Sierra Leone was once considered to have, thanks to its beautiful beaches and hospitable inhabitants, 'a real future as a tourist destination'. Though brief, these opening moments establish the tranquillity of the natural environment and the peaceful stability of domesticity in the village. This is a world that 'works', an Africa that functions peacefully by design. As I take up in the next section, Freetown is introduced to the audience as a place that is by definition threatening. Rural space, by contrast, is harmonious. It is apolitical and stable.

This makes the intrusion of the RUF forces moments later especially jarring. From the bush that surrounds Solomon and Dia Vandy emerges the sound of revving engines and hip hop. An instant later come the visuals of four-wheel-drive pick-ups loaded with rebel fighters. They are armed with AK-47s and a massive boom box. The audience's introduction to the RUF, like the Vandys', is decidedly abrupt, visually and narratively, and it registers as an offence against the natural tranquillity of the people and the place of the village. Zwick notes the importance of establishing early the horror of this war, hence both the suddenness and the savagery of the RUF attack. There is no contextualization of this violence. The text in the opening credits has stated that Sierra Leone is at war over diamonds, but when the RUF fighters appear they do so as an element out of place in the world that has been established in the first moments of the film. In contrast to the industrious, silently elegant fishermen, they are a marauding horde of gangstas: their music, dress, demeanour are all coded in ways that privilege global stereotypes of threatening black male youth.

What follows, then, is understood as mass criminality, not warfare. These young men set about destroying the village without commentary, killing indiscriminately and at close range. Many of their victims are women and children. In contrast to the later scenes of fighting in Freetown, their violence is methodical. Fighters are shown holding their weapons up, sighting them properly and then firing single shots or short bursts directly at their targets. Their violence is widespread and devastating, but it is carried out with precision and expertise. It comes across as both illegitimate and coldly calculated.

It is only once the initial wave of the assault is over that *Blood Diamond* introduces the idea that there may be a politics to what we have witnessed. Just as quickly, however, it wipes that possibility away. Those villagers captured by the RUF are lined up beneath the palm trees at the village centre. Captain Poison, the rebel unit's leader, commands his men to bring the villagers forward one by one to have their limbs amputated by young men swinging axes and machetes. 'Long sleeves or short sleeves?' each one is asked, meaning a cut at the wrist or above the elbow. While the deed is done by his 'boys', Captain Poison lets them know that the RUF is there to liberate the country, pulling from his pocket and then quickly replacing a small tattered pamphlet, presumably the group's manifesto. The amputation, he explains to the terrified villagers, is both punishment and pre-emption. The government's slogan for the upcoming

103

national elections is 'The Future Is in Your Hands'. But, Captain Poison tells a young man as he is prepared for amputation, 'We [the RUF] are the future. No more hands, no more voting'.

Much about this scene is derived from the actual practices of the RUF. Amputations and the rhetoric of 'short' and 'long sleeves' that accompanied them were a signature of the RUF (though there is some evidence that it was more widely practised by former members of the Sierra Leonean military than by the RUF proper). The exact reasons for the amputations have been debated by observers of the Sierra Leone war, but the connection to the Sierra Leone People's Party election slogan is obvious. The manifesto Captain Poison pulls from his pocket would seem to be a passing reference to the pamphlet 'Bushpaths to Democracy', which has been described as the RUF's most coherent ideological statement. Though mostly a vague mash-up of Frantz Fanon quotes and revolutionary-sounding rhetoric, 'Bushpaths to Democracy' did articulate a set of grievances around the way young people in Sierra Leone had been marginalized by the nation's ruling elites.

These gestures at a political position for the RUF, however poorly defined they may have been, are quickly subsumed under a larger narrative of greed. When Solomon Vandy is dragged to the chopping block and asked whether he prefers long or short sleeves, Captain Poison steps in at the last moment. 'Not this one,' he says as the machete is raised. 'Look at him. Put him in the truck. Bring him to the mines. He can work.' Whatever political statements the RUF may have been willing to inscribe on the bodies of rural villagers, they are secondary to the need for strong labour digging diamonds. The chapter ends with the trucks riding off with their captives, headed for the diamond fields of Kono.

The next chapter begins with a sudden shift in location from the ruptured idyll of rural Sierra Leone. Over the next several minutes the film alternates between the mines and a boardroom in Antwerp. 'Throughout the history of Africa,' intones the American representative to the G8 summit on conflict diamonds, 'whenever a substance of value is found, the locals die in great number and in misery'. The camera returns to Captain Poison, policing his captive workforce. Though he makes a few vague pronouncements about how the RUF is creating a new Sierra Leone with no masters and no slaves, these scenes revolve around his surveillance of the diggers. When one of them attempts to hide a small gem in his mouth, Captain Poison forces him to spit it out and then executes the man on the spot.

From this point forward there are no challenges to the portrayal of the RUF as nothing more than a criminal organization. In fact, the 'criminality' of the RUF is multifaceted. As Laura Chrisman (forthcoming) has argued, the rebels are doubly criminal because while they are animated by diamonds, they simultaneously fail to engage the trade as legitimate capitalists. The RUF's greed is not so much for the surplus profits of diamond wealth as it is for the means to produce more violence. One young commander, trading stones with Danny Archer, explains that he does not know what to do with all his accumulated diamonds beyond buying weapons, and the film makes repeated reference to Sierra Leonean's ignorance of the particulars of the global diamond trade.

War in the City

The RUF's unforeseen assault on the Vandys' seaside village stands in stark contrast to the slow build-up to the Freetown invasion. The eleventh chapter of the film, 'Freetown Siege', begins with a long shot of the sun rising over the city. Mist and smoke hover over the densely packed slums of the hillside. The shot foreshadows the final image of Freetown after the rebels have seized the city: the same long shot with buildings literally ablaze. There are no people in these images, just the ominous threatening presence of an overpopulated and underdeveloped urban tableau.

The RUF is 'introduced' in the next sequence through a BBC radio report (see Introduction, this volume, for more on the use of actual news media reports in fictional films). The British broadcaster announces the rebel presence some ten kilometres outside the city with dire warnings of an imminent attack. Uniformed security personnel take up positions on the street, lining up and harassing civilians for reasons that are not entirely clear but signal the tensions and stress of an encroaching war.[11] As Danny Archer and Solomon Vandy argue with one another outside the luxury hotel in which Vandy has found employment, there is a crack of small arms fire to mark the inevitably of urban war. The camera begins to circle Archer and Vandy standing toe to toe, building a sense of tension that culminates with an exploding vehicle and then, out of the smoke, the RUF vehicles re-appear.

What follows is, like the earlier representation of violence, decontextualized (see Eltringham, this volume). There is no stated reason for the RUF to attack Freetown. Aside from the brief and quickly forgotten gestures toward politics by Captain Poison, the war in Sierra Leone has been portrayed as entirely about the control of rural resources. Nothing in *Blood Diamond* suggests why the capital city is a desirable target for either capture or destruction. In fact, quite the opposite: to a criminal network interested only in profiteering from the diamond trade, attacking the city would be senseless and counter-productive. But whereas the idyllic portrait of the village makes the sudden eruption of violence seem illegitimate and criminal, the city is established as a place in which violence is endemic and natural. The portrait of the African city is a portrait of the inevitability of destruction, and the RUF attack is a foregone conclusion.

Visually, the Freetown invasion is a four-minute sequence of urban disintegration. Like the opening assault on the Vandys' village the editing is fast paced, a montage of intense violence (see Kapteijns, this volume, for a discussion of a similar 'excess of spectacle' in *Black Hawk Down*). But here both the camera work and the visual content are different. Much of this sequence is shot with hand held, mobile cameras. Zwick describes his desire in this scene in particular to capture the aesthetic of documentary films from the period, many of which were shot on small cameras from hidden positions. (Sorious Somora, the journalist who made *Cry Freetown* [2000], the most famous of these films, served as a technical consultant to *Blood Diamond*.) To enhance the newsreel effect, in at least some of these scenes the camera operators were not told how the action would unfold, leaving them to shoot as though they were photojournalists documenting unscripted news (see Introduction and Eltringham this volume, for a discussion of the 'restaging' of news media footage). The result is cacophonous. The blurred camera work and the action that slips fluidly into and out of the frame create a sense of total destruction, of violence that surrounds the camera (and hence the viewer) 360 degrees. There are occasional pauses allowing the audience to follow, for example, the trail of an RPG as it streaks towards a building. But for the most part it is impossible to focus on individual acts within this sequence. Figures pop into the frame and fire, or they drop to the ground after being hit. Except for the two rebels shot by Danny Archer as he and Vandy run through the city streets, it is almost impossible in any of these frames to visually connect a dying victim with the 'author' of his or her death. The rebels fire on the city as a whole. Unlike the methodical semi-professional gun play earlier in the film, the rebels in Freetown discharge in unfocused, sustained bursts. More often than not they shoot from the hip, gangsta style, rather than taking aim at their targets. As a consequence of visually disconnecting the rebels from dying Freetownians, the city itself seems to rain death as its residents attempt to flee. Cars, buildings and bodies simply explode. Men and women who are obviously not fighters themselves drop to the street or spray blood on the walls, literally coming apart along with their surroundings.

The culmination of these scenes of violence in Freetown's capital shows the rebels in control of the city. The visuals are of urban nightscapes lit by bonfires, Molotov cocktails and mortar flashes. Commandeered vehicles drag corpses through the streets while child soldiers drink grain alcohol and smoke brown-brown, Sierra Leonean fighters' fabled mixture of heroin and gunpowder. Young men dance through the streets in Halloween masks and pink wigs. The climax is a long shot of orange flame. Across the plane of the screen armed silhouettes dance around a pyre, seeming to sacrifice the city itself. The effect is to portray the city at war as a space of unimaginable and unmitigated catastrophe. 'What follows,' says Zwick in his commentary:

> I thought of more as a rave than anything else ...They [the rebels] were crazy. They were drunk on bloodlust. They had killed. They had exceeded any of the bounds of normative social behaviour. And so there they were, set free in this city where they had suddenly become the masters. And that's what this sequence just really became about. Just the craziest things we could think to do ... These anarchic kids were, at least for a brief moment, in charge of the entire society.

The echoes of Kaplan's portrait of the African city are striking. These are molecules at loose in an unstable social fluid. The fact that the RUF only briefly held parts of Freetown in the attack of 6 January 1999 is irrelevant from the point of view of *Blood Diamond*. The rebels' rave-like celebration is not meant to mark their success in combat. It is meant to illustrate the violent, asocial nature of the city. As Archer and Vandy slip beyond the borders of Freetown and begin a more conventional story of adventure and redemption, Freetown remains as the (urban) space of violence that cannot be redeemed and cannot, ultimately, be understood.

Circulations of Violence

In an examination of West African film, Dudley Andrew (2000: 227) writes that, 'Africa may destabilize conventional production, conventional imagery, and conventional film language, but Western notions always move in quickly to contain the continent's energy, usually pouring it into standard generic moulds'.

Though *Blood Diamond* gently challenged certain Hollywood conventions – by naming the African country in which it was set, by dealing with an historical rather than fictitious conflict, by challenging a powerful global industry – the filmmakers ultimately opted for most of the 'standard generic moulds' of Africa that circulate through Hollywood and through the global popular imaginary. The result is a representation of Africa that looks pleasingly and generically 'African'. The fungibilty of African spaces for the filmmakers, and by extension for much of the film's audience, is exemplified by the fact that whereas *Blood Diamond* is set primarily in West Africa, the majority of the film was shot in Mozambique and South Africa (see Eltringham, this volume). As a result, many of the rural scenes are a mash of Sierra Leonean backgrounds and southern African foregrounds. The urban landscapes of 'Freetown' in the film are a montage of Cape Town, Freetown and Maputo, cities with very different aesthetics that are clearly identifiable in the film. These errors are obvious to those familiar with the geographical differences of the African continent. Nevertheless, such a composite Africa does little to disrupt or challenge most of the films' audience, for whom Africa is a singular and largely un-nuanced unit (see Introduction, this volume, for a discussion of the 'geo-conflation' of Africa).

The two foundational moments of violence I have explored here, however, suggest that it is not enough to simply critique a film like *Blood Diamond* for the way it peddles 'acceptable' Hollywood stereotypes of the continent. There is a more interesting engagement to be made with the film, one that illuminates two simultaneously circulating and somewhat contradictory imaginaries about African violence: one urban, one rural. *Blood Diamond* takes these elements of the Sierra Leone war and flattens them out, reducing them to a level of abstraction. Whether *Blood Diamond* achieves much as an intervention into the trade from which it draws its name is debatable. But as a vehicle for understanding the Sierra Leone war itself, *Blood Diamond* is less useful for what it shows about the Sierra Leone war than the way it visualizes a set of global fantasies about violence in African space.

Notes

1. This and the other references to Zwick in this chapter are from the director's commentary on the DVD version of *Blood Diamond*.
2. See 'Hopeless Africa', *The Economist*, 11 May 2000. Retrieved 5 April 2011 from http://www.economist.com/node/333429
3. The most comprehensive histories of the war are Gberie (2005) and Keen

(2005). For more on the RUF in particular, see Abdullah (2004); Peters (2006); Richards (1996).
4. The AFRC was the Armed Forces Revolutionary Council, the faction of the Sierra Leone Army which overthrew the democratically elected government in 1997. The combined RUF/AFRC force renamed itself the People's Army, a name which was not widely taken up outside the force itself.
5. The Mende are the largest ethnic community in Sierra Leone, with much of the population concentrated in the south and east of the country.
6. On the racial politics at work in *Blood Diamond*, see Chrisman (forthcoming).
7. Krio is the English-based creole spoken in the capital, and to a lesser degree up-country. Krio also refers to the ethnic minority descended from slaves returned to the West African coast, a population that settled primarily in and around the Freetown peninsula.
8. Although the country in which *Beasts of No Nation* is set goes unnamed in the book, the backdrop is clearly contemporary Anglophone West Africa.
9. The Special Court for Sierra Leone was the war crimes tribunal established in 2002 by the United Nations and the government of Sierra Leone. Thirteen indictments were handed down to members of three factions and to Charles Taylor, at the time the President of neighboring Liberia. In an odd, Hollywood twist, Taylor's trial included testimony by the supermodel Naomi Campbell, who was alleged to have been given uncut Sierra Leonean diamonds by Taylor when the two met at a benefit in South Africa.
10. From the opening statement, 3 June 2004, Special Court for Sierra Leone Prosecutor David Crane: http://www.sc-sl.org/LinkClick.aspx?fileticket =wt7ALUTt4gk%3D&tabid=196. For more on this case and the depoliticization of the war, see Hoffman (2007) and Kelsall (2009).
11. The film's few depictions of uniformed, state soldiers represent one of *Blood Diamond*'s greatest exercises of poetic licence with the actual history of the war. Zwick argues that for narrative clarity the filmmakers decided to collapse into a single visual figure the Sierra Leone Army, the Nigerian-led peacekeeping force ECOMOG, the pro-government militias operating in Freetown and British paratroopers.

Filmography

Samora, S. (Dir.) 2000. *Cry Freetown* (London: Insight Television News).
Zwick, E. (Dir.) 2006. *Blood Diamond* (Warner Bros. Pictures, Virtual Studios, Spring Creek Productions, Bedford Falls Productions, Lonely Film Productions GmbH & Co. KG).

References

Abdullah, I. 2004. 'Bush Paths to Destruction: The Origin and Character of the Revolutionary United Front (RUF/SL)', in I. Abdullah (ed.), *Between Democracy and Terror: The Sierra Leone Civil War*. Dakar: CODESRIA, pp. 41–65.
Andrew, D. 2000. 'The Roots of the Nomadic: Gilles Deleuze and the Cineman of West Africa', in G. Flaxman (ed.), *The Brain is the Screen: Deleuze and the Philosophy of Cinema*. Minneapolis: University of Minnesota Press, pp. 215–249.
Campbell, G. 2002. *Blood Diamonds: Tracing the Path of the World's Most Precious Stones*. New York: Basic Books.
Chrisman, L. (forthcoming). 'The Sight, Sound, and Global Traffic in Blackness in *Blood Diamond*', *African Studies Review*.
Collier, P. 2000. 'Rebellion as a Quasi-Criminal Activity', *The Journal of Conflict Resolution* 44(6): 839–853.
Collier, P. and A. Hoeffler. 2000. *Greed and Grievance in Civil War*. World Bank Policy Research Working Paper No. 2355.
Fithen, D.C. 1999. 'Diamonds and War in Sierra Leone: Cultural Strategies for Commercial Adaptation to Endemic Low-Intensity Conflict', Ph.D. dissertation. London: Department of Anthropology, University College London.
Gberie, L. 2005. *A Dirty War in West Africa: The RUF and the Destruction of Sierra Leone*. Bloomington, IN: Indiana University Press.
Hoffman, D. 2004. 'The Civilian Target in Sierra Leone and Liberia: Political Power, Military Strategy, and Humanitarian Intervention', *African Affairs* 103(411): 211–26.
———. 2007. 'The Meaning of a Militia: Understanding the Civil Defence Forces of Sierra Leone', *African Affairs* 106(425): 639–62.
Iweala, U. 2005. *Beasts of No Nation*. New York: Harper Collins.
Kandeh, J. 1996. 'What Does the "Militariat" Do When it Rules? Military Regimes: The Gambia, Sierra Leone and Liberia', *Review of African Political Economy* 23(69): 387–404.
Kaplan, R. 2000. *The Coming Anarchy: Shattering the Dreams of the Post Cold War*. New York: Vintage.
Keen, D. 2005. *Conflict and Collusion in Sierra Leone*. New York: Palgrave.
Kelsall, T. 2009. *Culture under Cross-Examination: International Justice and the Special Court for Sierra Leone*. New York: Cambridge University Press.
Peters, K. 2006. 'Footpaths to Reintegration: Armed Conflict, Youth and the Rural Crisis in Sierra Leone', Ph.D. dissertation. Wageningen: Wageningen University.
Rashid, I. 2004. 'Student Radicals, Lumpen Youth, and the Origins of Revolutionary Groups in Sierra Leone, 1977–1996', in I. Abdullah (ed.),

Between Democracy and Terror: The Sierra Leone Civil War. Dakar: CODESRIA, pp. 66–89.

Reno, W. 1995. *Corruption and State Politics in Sierra Leone*. Cambridge: Cambridge University Press.

Reno, W. 2003. 'Political Networks in a Failing State: The Roots and Future of Violent Conflict in Sierra Leone', *Internationale Politik und Gesellschaft [International Politics and Society]* 2: 44–66.

Richards, P. 1996. *Fighting for the Rainforest: War, Youth and Resources in Sierra Leone*. Portsmouth, NH: James Currey Press.

———. 1999. 'New Political Violence in Africa: Secular Sectarianism in Sierra Leone', *GeoJournal* 47(3): 433–42.

United States Department of the Army. 2003. *Urban Operations Field Manual*, FM3–06. Leavenworth, KS: U.S. Department of the Army.

Five

Showing What Cannot Be Imagined
Shooting Dogs and *Hotel Rwanda*[1]

Nigel Eltringham

How is one 'to show what cannot even be imagined?' asks the Holocaust survivor Elie Wiesel (1978) at the end of a critical review of the TV mini-series *Holocaust* (1978). Whatever the answer, filmmakers remain intent on telling stories of genocide. Keir Pearson (2005: 15, 20), the screenwriter for *Hotel Rwanda* (2004), felt it 'was a story that had to be told', while the film's director, Terry George (2005: 23, 25), recalls a visit, a year before the film was shot, to the Murambi genocide memorial in Southern Rwanda and writing in the visitor's book, 'I promise to tell the story of the genocide to the world'. Likewise, David Belton, the BBC journalist who reported from Rwanda in May 1994 and co-wrote the original story for *Shooting Dogs* (2005, renamed *Beyond the Gates* in the U.S.) has stated 'I wanted to come back and this time get the story out to a wider audience' (Walker 2004). However sincere their motives, filmmakers must still grapple with Wiesel's seemingly irresolvable dilemma; 'How is one to tell a tale that cannot be – but must be – told?' Alternatively, is this a dilemma experienced only by survivors like Wiesel or those who possess specialist knowledge of the events portrayed? Will these constituencies always remain dissatisfied with the outcome? Or, should the survivor and 'expert' accept that distortion, compression and caricature will be the price of mass pedagogy? *Hotel Rwanda* tells the story of the 1994 Rwandan genocide through the eyes of a real-life person, Paul Rusesabagina (Don Cheadle), who, together with his wife Tatiana (Sophie Okonedo) uses his position as a hotel manager, put in charge of the Hôtel des Milles Collines soon after the start of the genocide in April 1994, to save the lives of around 1,268 refugees. Constant attacks on the hotel result in an aborted attempt at evacuation organized by Colonel Oliver (Nick Nolte), loosely based on the UNAMIR (United Nations Assistance Mission for Rwanda) commander Romeo Dallaire. The climax of the film is a successful evacuation of the hotel. The screenplay was based on interviews with survivors and Rusesabagina (Pearson 2005: 14–21). *Shooting Dogs*, by contrast, concerns three fictional characters – Father Christopher (John Hurt), Joe Conner (Hugh Dancy) and Marie (Clare-Hope Ashitey) – in a factual context: the abandonment by UN peacekeepers of refugees at the Ecole Technique Officielle (ETO) in Kigali (Des Forges 1999: 613–18). Father Christopher and Joe Conner give sanctuary to two thousand refugees, protected by soldiers of the Belgian contingent of UNAMIR, from surrounding *Interahamwe* militia. When the UN soldiers evacuate, Joe leaves with them, the school is overrun by the militia and the refugees are murdered. Christopher is later killed by a militia member at a roadblock. The original treatment was written by David Belton, who reported for the BBC from Rwanda during the genocide.

Both films adopt a classical realist form; the illusion of experiencing not discordant memory or a mediated narrative, but 'mastery over the past', the authentic reproduction of reality (Hirsch 2004: 3) whereby the image becomes 'no more than a window onto unmediated "reality"' (Rosenstone 1992: 507; see Sontag 2003: 46). This is in contrast to other films that have sought to tell a story of genocide. Sidney Lumet's *The Pawnbroker* (1964), for example, emulates the fragmented, 'durational time' (Langer 1997: 55) of traumatic memory by embedding a Holocaust survivor's flashbacks within a conventional linear narrative. An alternative device is the trial, as seen in Peter Weiss's (Weiss and Gross 1966) Auschwitz play, *The Investigation*, in which the audience is forced to confront the ethical and epistemological dilemmas of constructing a coherent narrative from discontinuous and often contradictory fragments. Such *indirect* portrayal of mass murder is not only sensitive to Wiesel's (1978) concern as to how one is 'to show what cannot even be imagined', but also endorses Allen Feldman's (2000: 59) recognition that the visual realism of cinema imposes (inadvertently) a coercive, omniscient singularity that replicates the 'realist scopic regime' essential to regimes of domination and violence. Such indirect portrayal, it has been argued, avoids the 'deceptive immediacy' of the realist narrative and increases the 'potential for genuine ethical witness' (Gregory 2006: 203).

Where *The Pawnbroker* and *The Investigation* convey reality through fragments (requiring the audience to actively interpret and thereby appreciate contingency) the classical realist forms of *Hotel Rwanda* and *Shooting Dogs* 'show' reality to the audience as if it were an unmediated history. Terry George (2006) concedes, however, that '[t]o make a film of a true story you must compress timelines, create composite characters and dramatize emotions'. Does such temporal and agentive compression make *Shooting Dogs* and *Hotel Rwanda* deficient as 'history'? As discussed in the Introduction to this volume, both written history and realist film rely on the 'fiction that the past itself can be truly told in neat, linear stories' (Rosenstone 1992: 508). Both genres abbreviate and compress. Neither is able to convey the past in a comprehensive way. It would be disingenuous, therefore, to evaluate films according to stricter criteria than we evaluate historical writing.

No film or written historical account can be exhaustively omniscient, dealing with all possible aspects, but must ask a particular question regarding an event or series of events (Eaglestone 2001: 28; Hirsch 1995: 18). Books about the Rwandan genocide have, for example, focused on perpetrators (Hatzfeld 2005; Straus 2006); the role of the church (Longman 2009); the role of the United Nations (Barnett 2002; Melvern 2000); and the role of the media (Chrétien et al. 1995). Film does not, of course, have the luxury of parsing the genocide in this intrinsically artificial manner. *Shooting Dogs* and *Hotel Rwanda*, for example, must touch on all these issues (and more) but cannot hope to deal with any of them exhaustively. As Beata, a Rwandan genocide survivor observed following the Kigali premier of *Shooting Dogs*, 'I cannot expect people to know everything – it is so unimaginable, so incomprehensible. Show me a film about the Holocaust that is totally factual and conveys it all' (Milmo 2006).

We should not, therefore, evaluate these films according to an erroneous understanding of written history as 'something solid and unproblematic', but concede that written history, like film, 'is never a mirror [of reality] but a construction' (Rosenstone 2000: 52). While these films exhibit 'narrative fetishism' (Santner 1992: 144) (requiring compression, abbreviation etc.) it can be argued that these concessions are necessary to create a film 'capable of efficiently communicating a set of historical facts to a mass audience' (Hirsch 2004: 25). As Michael Caton-Jones, the director of *Shooting Dogs* observes, 'There is always an essential compromise to ensure the film does its job' (Milmo 2006).

There is, however, a need for caution when a film avidly proclaims its authenticity. Despite the fact its three central characters are fictional, the opening title of *Shooting Dogs* reads: 'THIS FILM IS BASED ON REAL EVENTS AND WAS MADE AT THE LOCATION DEPICTED'. The *proximity* of the reconstruction to the events and place is emphasized implying an 'unmediated *immediacy*' (Duage-Roth 2010: 172). What should an audience make of this statement? Another genocide film, *Conspiracy* (2001), is also a recreation of 'real events' (the January 1942 Wannsee conference at which the 'Final Solution of the Jewish Problem' was planned) and was filmed at the 'location depicted' (the villa at 56–58 Am Grossen Wannsee in Berlin). On one hand, the viewer assumes that the formal proceedings depicted in *Conspiracy* are 'as they happened', for the opening narration tells us, 'Only one record of what was said and done here survives'; we are shown the stenographer and the film ends with the caption 'Martin Luther's copy of the Wannsee Conference minutes was discovered in ... 1947. It is the only record of the meeting that survives'. While one assumes that the viewer will realize that casual conversations away from the conference table are embellishments, necessary to externalize the inner motivations of characters, the viewer is directed to believe that the formal discussions are verbatim. And yet, this is an example of the blurring of record versus conjecture, for the Wannsee Protocol (the conference's minutes) is not a verbatim record: *all the exchanges in the film are conjecture*; '[t]here is no camera-eye view' of the proceedings (Roseman 2003: 4). Even an ostensibly real-time film based on written 'minutes' relies on conjecture to achieve its 'reality effect'.

In contrast to *Conspiracy*, in which an actual written record is extensively embellished, *Hotel Rwanda* and *Shooting Dogs* rely on an amalgam of eyewitness testimony. The screenwriter of *Hotel Rwanda* has stated: 'Weeks were filled hearing hundreds of hours of testimonials from countless survivors from all walks of life' (Pearson 2005: 20). The use of eyewitness accounts also bolsters claims to 'authenticity'. But, conflated testimony is of a different order from atomized eyewitness testimony. No eyewitness experiences an event in its entirety (Jay 1992: 104) and to reconstruct a meaningful narrative requires a wider view than that accessible to a single eyewitness (Haidu 1992: 294): an artificial resolution of the 'meanwhile' and the 'elsewhere' of experience (Errington 1979: 239). And there is also the question of which eyewitnesses were consulted. While Elie Wiesel (Cargas 1986: 5) suggests that '[a]ny survivor has more to say than all the historians combined about what happened', he draws a distinction between knowledge retrievable from an extant text and/or survivor-witness with the irretrievable 'philosophical knowledge' of the victim's final encounter with her or his killer (see Levi 1989: 63–64). While the dead cannot be consulted, the killer's side of that encounter is retrievable (Hatzfeld 2005; Mironko 2006;

117

Straus 2006). Despite this, the perpetrators in *Shooting Dogs* remain silent as regards motivation (see below). Beyond the need to evaluate these two films according to a nuanced appreciation of professional history and be wary of claims to authenticity ('Based on Real Events and was Made at the Location Depicted') there is the question of whether 'factual inaccuracies' are accidental or intentional and the extent to which they undermine a film's pedagogical purpose.

Questions of Accuracy

Questions of 'accuracy' can be considered in two main groupings: the minor (intentional or unintentional) and intentional revisions (see Leopold, this volume). In *Hotel Rwanda*, for example, the vehicles are right-hand drive because the film was shot in South Africa due to government funding (contributing to the 'geo-conflation of "Africa"' – see Introduction and Hoffman, this volume). Similarly, Colonel Oliver is a Canadian, but uses the American pronunciation of 'lieutenant'. And yet, such 'inaccuracies' are excusable, for as Daniel Walkowitz (1985) states, 'I am less concerned ... whether the shoes are authentic – than with the pattern of a set of social relationships' portrayed.

There are, however, intentional revisions/inventions. In the evacuation scene in *Hotel Rwanda*, it is Colonel Oliver (loosely based on General Romeo Dallaire) who diffuses the stand-off with the *Interahamwe*. Amadou Deme (2006), a Senegalese member of UNAMIR present at the aborted evacuation, has criticized the film because Dallaire was not present and it was Georges Rutaganda (vice-president of the *Interahamwe*) who talked down the 'murderous mob'. As regards *Shooting Dogs*, no white priest stayed behind at the ETO and no white priest was killed by the *Interahamwe* – although a Spanish priest, Joaquín Valmajo, was killed by the Rwandan Patriotic Army in April 1994 (Des Forges 1999: 711). David Belton (British Film Institute 2005a) has explained that Father Christopher is based on a Bosnian priest, Vjeko Curic, who protected Belton and his BBC colleagues during the genocide and who sheltered many Tutsi and helped them to escape to Burundi. Curic was murdered in Kigali by unknown assailants in 1998.[2] However, as Grace, a survivor of the ETO massacre stated having seen the film, 'It is a good film but I am a little confused. I don't remember this young man who was the teacher. And the priests were Belgians. They left with the United Nations. It is not quite as it happened. Was what really happened not enough?' (Milmo 2006). These inventions correspond to Robert Rosenstone's (2000: 62) idea of the 'true' invention which condenses or symbolizes what is attested to in other sources (see Introduction, this volume). In other words, General Dallaire did confront the *Interahamwe* (Dallaire and Beardsley 2003: 369), just not on the occasion portrayed in *Hotel Rwanda* and there was a white priest who saved many Tutsi (Vjeko Curic) although not at the ETO. And yet, the degree to which one assigns verity to these inventions depends on one's personal location. As a member of the audience I am not troubled by these inventions, but they clearly trouble Amadou and Grace and that is a tension cannot be easily resolved.

Knowledge acquired from direct experience is one personal location which leads to dissatisfaction with 'invented' elements. Knowledge gained through detailed research is another. Shortly after the genocide it was observed that the 'Western media's failure to report [the genocide adequately] possibly contributed to international indifference and inaction, and hence the crime itself' (Adelman, Suhrke and Jones 1996). Linda Melvern, who has written extensively on international failure during the genocide (Melvern 2000), has criticized *Shooting Dogs'* 'shocking disregard for the historical record' because it portrays a BBC TV crew at the ETO between 7 and 11 April 1994 when no BBC crew was in Rwanda at the time. Melvern also notes that although a BBC journalist (Nicola Walker) is portrayed saying (around 7 April) to the Belgian UNAMIR Captain (Dominique Horwitz), 'Some people are starting to call this a genocide. Would you call it that?' No BBC news report used the term 'genocide' until 29 April 1994 (see Keane 2006 for a response).

Beyond the question of 'invention' (true or otherwise) is the question of a film's internal coherence, or 'indexicality' (Garfinkel 1967: 4–5) – the sense that each moment of a film's narrative only possesses meaning because of relations with other narrative moments. The concern then shifts from the issue of elements (irrespective of whether they are 'true', condensing inventions), to absences *between* elements. Thirty minutes into *Shooting Dogs*, for example, a man calling himself 'Ngulinzira' seeks shelter at the ETO, introducing himself to the Belgian UNAMIR Captain and Christopher as 'a former minister of this so-called government'. Earlier in the film, however, the BBC journalist states that in Rwanda 'you've got a government that says all Tutsi are scum'. So why is a minister seeking sanctuary? After the minister's arrival, 'Councillor Sibomana' tells Christopher that ten Belgian soldiers have been 'kidnapped while guarding our Prime Minister' and a few moments later the Belgian Captain tells Christopher the Prime Minister has been murdered. No explanation, however, is given for why a minister would seek sanctuary or why the Prime Minister has been murdered and the audience is not told that the Prime Minister (Agathe Uwilingiyimana) was a Hutu. Here, the filmmakers missed an opportunity to convey an important message about the nature of the genocide and the fantasy of ethnicity propagated by extremists. The government in place on 6 April was composed of the internal Hutu opposition who, under constant attack from extremist factions including the Coalition pour la défense de la République, had negotiated the 1993 Arusha Accords (a power-sharing agreement) with the predominantly Tutsi Rwandan Patriotic Front (RPF) (Eltringham 2004: 81–97). Having been denounced as *ibyitso* ('RPF collaborators'), many of the members of the government were targeted within the first few hours of the genocide (including Agathe Uwilingiyimana). This was a complex political landscape, but conveying a sense of that complexity is essential to undermine the extremists' fantasy of society divided into 'Hutu' and 'Tutsi' and the post-genocide binaries of 'victim-Tutsi' and 'perpetrator-Hutu'. Something of this complexity could have been conveyed had the BBC journalist not been given the line 'you've got a government that says all Tutsi are scum' (which was not the case on 5 April 1994); had the fictionalized minister been described as a Hutu; and had it been made clear that the Prime Minister was a Hutu. Instead, this opportunity is missed. Furthermore, the Belgian UNAMIR Captain characterizes the Arusha peace process as 'We are here to monitor the peace *between Hutu and Tutsi*', rather than monitoring peace between the internal Hutu opposition government and the RPF in a context in which an extremist Hutu faction was undermining a fragile peace established by a Hutu opposition and a Tutsi-dominated RPF. As Alexandre Duage-Roth (2010: 171) suggests, 'The moment these cinematic representations offer a vision of the past, they also mask and exclude certain facets of the history to which they bear witness and ... institute a form of forgetting, if not illegitimate revisionism of history'.

Replacing the Missing Image of Death

Both *Hotel Rwanda* and *Shooting Dogs* use broadcasts made by the international media (see Introduction, this volume). Both films, for example, use the press conference given by Christine Shelley (U.S. State Department spokesperson) on 28 April 1994 in which she declined to apply the term 'genocide' to Rwanda in an unqualified way. Audio of the press conference appears about halfway into *Hotel Rwanda* (as if it was a radio broadcast), while in *Shooting Dogs* the actual footage is shown at the end of the film (although it is not made clear who the speaker is or for whom she is speaking).

In *Hotel Rwanda,* however, media footage is used in a particular way. It is important to recall that of the mass murder of the Holocaust there is only one known piece of film, lasting about two minutes, shot in Latvia in 1941 (Hirsch 2004: 1). The same applies to the Rwandan genocide, of which there are only three videos of actual killing (see Hughes 2007). One was shot by the British journalist Nick Hughes, who describes the footage in *The Hunger Business* (2000):[3]

I was at the top of the French School and two women, I think probably a mother and daughter, sitting in a pile of bodies, pleading for their lives and some of the bodies weren't dead and they were still being violently beaten, really tortured to death. Amongst all these bodies people were still walking around in pairs talking, even going shopping, even going about their normal life as they stepped over these people who had been killed.

In his discussion of films about the Holocaust, Joshua Hirsch (2004: 21) notes that because '[r]ealism abhors a vacuum; it converts the absence of the past into a visible presence' and filmmakers replace 'the missing image of death'. But, something else happens in *Hotel Rwanda*. Forty minutes into the film the journalist Jack Daglish (Joaquin Phoenix) walks into a hotel room where his boss, David (David O'Hara), puts a VHS tape into the player. David asks, 'What is this?' Jack says nothing; images need no explanation. The audience sees the monitor on which is playing a recreation of Nick Hughes' footage, although the viewpoint is closer than the original. Here, therefore, there is a triple mediation – real footage; re-created; shown on a screen; within a screen. David [on the phone] says, 'I've got incredible footage. It's a massacre, dead bodies, machetes. If I get this through right away can you make the evening news? You have to lead with this'. The camera then cuts away and returns to the monitor, but this time the monitor fills the screen and just as our perspective is closer to the monitor so the footage on the monitor zooms in on the dead bodies and men holding machetes, a proximity that does not exist in Nick Hughes's footage. The shot on the monitor then pans back and ends at the same proximity as it had at the start, the same proximity as Nick Hughes's original footage.

Here, the otherwise realist film does not simply recreate a 'missing image of death' (Hirsch 2004: 21), but recreates what was recorded and broadcast, placing it outside the stream of realism. Is this an attempt to reduce horror? Terry George, the director of *Hotel Rwanda*, has stated: 'I did not want anyone to feel that they should avoid this film because it was gory and it would be distasteful to watch' (DVD interview). This raises the question of whether showing a re-creation of footage that many in the audience may already have seen and in a format they are familiar with (watching it on TV) is a way of reducing 'distaste'. In other words, by mediating violence in a way familiar to the audience – watching a TV report, which evokes distance rather than the emotional investment demanded in the rest of the film – is the unimaginable made familiar?

Surrogates and Empathy

Elie Wiesel (1978) criticized *Holocaust* for its 'contrived situations [and] sentimental episodes'. Andreas Huyssen (1980: 123), however, argues that it was precisely this 'emotional and personal identification' with a particular family that explained the impact of the series. Through long exposure to film, audiences anticipate emotional identification with specific characters (Torchin 2006: 217), which often involve: suspicion about those in positions of power; 'the struggle of the little person versus the big one, the weaker versus the powerful'; and the 'exceptional individual' who fights authority and anonymous forces (Toplin 1996: 12–13). All of these devices are present in *Hotel Rwanda* and *Shooting Dogs*.

It has been argued that this cinematic device of emotional identification with specific characters tends to crowd out consideration of more complex historical and social factors (see Rosenstone 1992: 507; Toplin 1996: 20). Just as the criminal trials of those who commit genocide concentrate on the minutia of the individual's actions rather than broader questions of why and how a genocide took place (Arendt 1994[1963]: 5), so a film that concentrates on the actions of individuals may fail to give due attention to broader questions of socio-historical context (see above). On the other hand, however, there is a confluence between these cinematic conventions and advocacy for victims of mass atrocity. Richard Rorty (1998: 122–27), for example, argues that in the context of mass atrocity we should 'concentrate our energies on manipulating sentiments' in order to 'expand the reference of the term ... "people like us"' so

123

that viewers 'imagine themselves in the shoes of the despised and oppressed'. *Hotel Rwanda*, for example, has been praised because 'we experience things through the eyes of one of the oppressed instead of having them mediated via the sensibility of European or America visitors' (French 2005). And yet, by implicitly criticizing films set in Africa with European lead characters, this comment misses something particular about Paul Rusesabagina. With a Hutu father and a Tutsi mother (Rusesabagina and Zoellner 2006: 26) Rusesabagina is a Hutu (following the patrilineal system), but is also an *ibiymanyi* (of mixed parentage). Although this is not mentioned in the film, it is made clear that Paul's wife is Tutsi and, therefore, his children are of mixed parentage like their father. The value of placing Rusesabagina at the centre of the narrative is not so much that he is a Rwandan rather than a European, but that as a Hutu with a Tutsi mother and a Tutsi wife he exposes the absurdity of the *génocidaire*'s racial discourse and the absurdity of those who would assign collective guilt to 'the Hutu'.

In contrast, *Shooting Dogs* has been criticized for its two non-African lead characters, because it 'is an African tragedy seen through outside eyes' (Mackie 2006) which may risk reproducing the 'heroic figure of the white man rescuing the African' (Duage-Roth 2010: 183). An encounter with genocide should confront an audience with 'a great many existential questions that we manage to avoid in our daily living' (Laub 1992: 72); questions concerning our mortality, losing loved ones, and the illusion of our individual omnipotence. The issue, then, is who is the intended audience to be confronted with these questions? The director, Michael Caton-Jones has argued, 'It's told through the eyes of Westerners because there is no point telling the Rwandans. They know what happened. My job is to tell the story to the West so that they will understand' (Walker 2004). Along the same lines, David Belton has explained that he wished to confront the Euro-American with the genocide, not the Rwandan, that '[he] didn't feel qualified to write a story from a specifically Rwandan perspective. The white man's role in Rwanda is so integral to what happened there in 1994' (British Film Institute

2005a). If one accepts that the purpose of the film is pedagogical, then placing a non-Rwandan as a central character allows situations in which the outsider's superficial knowledge and assumptions can be revealed and challenged, and complexity, hopefully, conveyed. Joe Conner, therefore, takes the audience's place as an uninformed surrogate: we learn as he learns. At times this device can stretch credulity. For example, Marie: 'There were *Interahamwe* in the streets.' Joe: '*Intera-* what?' And yet, as our main surrogate, Joe Conner's perspective gradually converges with the audience's *prospective* awareness of the enormity of the events unfolding; for after all, the audience knows the outcome (Levi 1989; Mackie 2006).[4] The contrast of Conner's foreboding with Christopher's resigned nonchalance heightens the audience's identification with the former because we know he is right. When Christopher later concedes, 'I have not seen this before,' the perspectives of the audience and its two surrogates become unified, enhancing identification.

Both films, irrespective of whether the lead characters are Rwandan, involve sieges, which also enhance audience identification with surrogates. Michael Jackson (2002: 33) observes that 'the intelligibility of any story or journey will depend on [the] unconscious bodily rhythm of going out from some place of certainty or familiarity into a space of contingency and strangeness, then returning to take stock'. Likewise, Joshua Hirsch (2004: 21) suggests that realist cinema enables us to experience 'history vicariously, on the condition of being free to return again unscathed' to our exterior position. This oscillation exists within the films. The audience's surrogates are exposed in measured doses to a reality happening outside (reflected in the fact that *Shooting Dogs* was renamed *Beyond the Gates* for its U.S. release). The Hôtel des Milles Collines and the ETO act as places of reflection for the viewer, to which we, who accompany our surrogates, can return and 'take stock', having been exposed to the shocking reality of the genocide outside:

Hotel Rwanda
Jack Daglish: David, the shit's going down outside these walls, we've gotta cover it.

Shootings Dogs
Christopher: I'll be alright.
Joe Conner: You won't be alright. I've been out there and it's falling apart.

Our surrogates venture out so that we may venture into horror, but we are never left in the midst of the genocide; the audience is not asked to endure terror beyond its imagination. And yet, achieving 'sentimental' identification through individual surrogates is not without dilemmas. It has been argued that the phenomenon of 'sad sentimental stories' as a literary genre in Western societies feeds a desire for sensation among those who consider themselves jaded and desensitized (Schaffer and Smith 2004: 13–14; see Ball 2000; Farrell 1998). But the response to being exposed to such images and accounts is unpredictable, leading to 'A call for peace. A cry for revenge. Or simply the bemused awareness ... that terrible things happen' (Sontag 2003: 11). Perhaps more important is Rorty's (1998: 113) recognition that one of the 'ways in which we paradigmatic humans distinguish ourselves from borderline cases' is to locate and rescue emblems of ourselves from the midst of those unlike ourselves. We require the presence of those with whom we do not identify to distinguish those emblems with which we do empathize (see Torchin 2006: 217). One of the ways that differentiation is achieved is by portraying unsympathetic/repulsive characters in a superficial, anonymous way, lacking the depth of the audience's surrogates. In its portrayal of the *Interahamwe*, for example, *Shooting Dogs* replicates media representation of Africans as a 'frantic mass' (Malkki 1996: 387). This precludes the recognition that each anonymous member of the *Interahamwe*, just like each anonymous Tutsi refugee sheltering in the ETO, has 'a name, opinions, relatives, and histories ... reasons for being where he [*sic*] is now'. As Michela Wrong (2005) observes, 'A film about Rwanda's genocide that doesn't grapple with the impenetrable riddle of how ordinary, decent folk were persuaded to do such extraordinary, indecent things has fallen at the first fence'. Although grappling with this question and humanizing perpetrators (Hatzfeld 2005; Mironko 2006; Straus 2006) may not be possible in a film (and may be unpalatable outside scholarly attempts to account for mass atrocity) we must remain conscious that to humanize surrogates may involve stripping others of what makes them human. As Rorty (1998: 126), speaking in the context of the former Yugoslavia, reminds us: 'We ... feel about the Serbian torturers and rapists as they feel about their Muslim victims'. There is a danger, therefore, that if the viewers of *Shooting Dogs* envisage themselves as 'real humans' contra the 'perverted' *Interahamwe*, this replicates the way that the *Interahamwe* considered themselves 'real humans' contra Tutsi, who they considered to be 'snakes', 'hyenas', 'dogs' and 'cockroaches'.

Despite this, both films contain direct messages to the audience challenging the place of Africans in the audience's 'universe of moral obligation' (Fein 1993: 43) (see Introduction, this volume). In *Hotel Rwanda*, when Colonel Oliver tells Paul that the recently arrived French soldiers will only evacuate 'whites', he states, 'You'd own this fucking hotel, except for one thing. You're fucking black! You're not even a nigger, you're African! They're not staying to stop this thing. They're gonna fly right out of here with their people'. More striking is the scene in *Shooting Dogs* in which the BBC journalist Rachel states, 'Anytime I saw a dead Bosnian woman, a white woman, I thought ... that could be my mum. Over here they're just dead Africans'. Here, the film's own device of generating audience empathy with European lead characters is implicitly challenged through a challenge to the audience's relationship with media images of violence in Africa.

The Social Life of Films

> The photographer's intentions do not determine the meaning of the photograph, which will have its own career, blown by the whims and loyalties of the diverse communities that have use for it. (Sontag 2003: 35)

While it was not until 1964 and the release of *The Pawnbroker* that the Holocaust (in the form of a concentration camp) was actually

127

portrayed, and even then only in flashback,[5] *Shooting Dogs* and *Hotel Rwanda* were made only ten years after the 1994 genocide. As indicated above, the writers and directors felt duty-bound to 'tell the story'. But, such 'historical' stories (like individual memory) are always determined by the ideological conditions and social needs of the present (see Eltringham 2004: 158–60; Hirsch 2004: 11; Santner 1992: 143) As Maurice Halbwachs demonstrated, 'even at the moment of reproducing the past our imagination remains under the influence of the present social milieu' (quoted in Halbwachs and Coser 1992: 49). The present, of course, is ephemeral and new histories can be written that reinterpret traces of the past according to the social and political needs of the present. In this way, historical representation parallels individual narrative memory which, as externalized event, displays a flexibility, able to respond to 'changes depending on the social conditions [of] a specific instance of remembering' (Hirsch 2004: 22; Zur 1997: 68). As ossified accounts, however, films are incapable of responding to the changing needs of the present. Frozen, immune to alteration, they are condemned to eternal repetition. In a sense, films can become traumatic memories, 'fixed and inflexible … literal recordings of past traumatic perceptions' (Hirsch 2004: 22) which freeze the past into an object of spectatorship (Feldman 2004: 165).

And the demands of the present do change. In 2003 Paul Rusesabagina returned to Rwanda (he had gone into self-imposed exile in 1996 following an attack on his home by a Tutsi soldier). Terry George (2005: 24) recalls: 'As he stepped off the plane in Kigali, Paul was mobbed by friends and family. At the Hôtel des Milles Collines, the staff rushed to hug the man who had saved their lives. Everywhere we went, Paul and Tatiana were greeted as heroes'. On the release of the film, genocide survivors described *Hotel Rwanda* as 'a very important film in terms of helping people learn more about what happened in Rwanda. It is accurate' (Cowley 2005) and at a private screening in May 2005 the Rwandan President, Paul Kagame, told Terry George that the film had 'done much good around the world in exposing the horrors of the genocide' (George 2006). When Rusesabagina criticized Paul Kagame's government in his autobiography (Rusesabagina and Zoellner 2006: 253–55), Kagame responded that it was it was not true that Rusesabagina was a hero who had saved hundreds of lives and that 'someone is trying to rewrite the history of Rwanda and we cannot accept it'.[6] In November 2006 Rusesabagina wrote a letter to the Prosecutor of the International Criminal Tribunal for Rwanda calling on him to investigate and prosecute 'war crimes, crimes against humanity and crimes of genocide, committed by General Paul Kagame and his army before and after 1994' (Rusesabagina 2006). In May 2007 an article entitled 'Paul Rusesabagina the self-declared saviour, treacherous liar' appeared in *The New Times* (an English-language Rwandan newspaper closely connected to the government) stating that Rusesabagina's 'revisionist and negationist theories clearly prove his links with *génocidaires* and Genocide ideology' (Mugabo 2007). Finally, in 2008, a book, co-authored by Kagame's public relations advisor, was published containing interviews with survivors who had sort shelter in the Hôtel des Milles Collines. The authors state that the survivor's 'accounts leave no room for doubt: the character in the film bears no resemblance whatsoever to the individual they knew' (Ndahiro and Rutazibwa 2008: 13). This rejection of *Hotel Rwanda* is primarily due to Rusesabagina's high-profile criticism of the government. As Lars Waldorf (2009: 114–18) demonstrates, before the film and autobiography the essentials of Rusesabagina's conduct (if not the film's embellishments) were independently recorded and corroborated.

In one way, this controversy (and others) could be seen as an 'act of remembrance', for such debates challenge the idea that the genocide is a distant historical event that can be reduced to a hundred minutes or so of celluloid. The genocide is not, and never will be, a distant historical event for survivors. This controversy also suggests a different reading of Wiesel's (1978: 119) dilemma, 'How is one to tell a tale that cannot be – but must be – told?' Perhaps it is not the telling of the tale, but the heat and light of debate that it generates that is a film's true pedagogical achievement. Terry George has stated that he wanted *Hotel Rwanda* to 'generate discussion and for people to learn from it' (Cowley 2005) while Michel Caton-Jones has stated that in directing *Shooting Dogs*, he wanted to 'shine a light on [the genocide], then people could go and educate themselves about it' (British Film Institute 2005b). It is hoped that audiences will do this. Maybe then they will appreciate Wiesel's comment on the Holocaust: 'The more I read about it, the less I understand it' (Cargas 1986: 5).

Notes

1. An earlier version of this chapter appeared as Eltringham, N. 2008, 'Besieged history? An evaluation of Shooting Dogs' *Environment and Planning D: Society and Space*, 26(4): 740–46. Published by Pion Limited, London.
2. See http://vjeko-rwanda.info
3. See also the documentary *Iseta: Behind the Roadblock*, which focuses on the identities and destinies of the victims filmed by Hughes.
4. As Haim Gouri (2004) comments, on watching German newsreels of Auschwitz at the Eichmann trial: 'As in the movies, you have the impulse to warn the hero "Look out behind you! Look out behind you!" The audience, after all, always knows things the actors do not.'
5. Anker, D. 2004. 'Imaginary Witness": Hollywood and the Holocaust,' in *Storyville* 92 min. USA.
6. See 'Rwanda President Kagame: International Criminal Tribunal For Rwanda "Not Properly Handling" Job', in *Voice of America*, 2006. Retrieved 1 November 2011 from http://www.insidevoa.com/media-relations/press-releases/a-13-34-2006-06-01-kagame-111608109.html

Filmography

Caton-Jones, M. (Dir.) 2005. *Shooting Dogs* (CrossDay Productions Ltd., ARTE, BBC Films, Egoli Tossell Film, Filmstiftung Nordrhein-Westfalen, Invicta Capital, UK Film Council, Zweites Deutsches Fernsehen (ZDF)).
George, T. (Dir.). 2004. *Hotel Rwanda* (United Artists).
Kabera, E. and J. Reina (Dirs) 2008. *Iseta: Behind the Roadblock* (Vivid Features).
Lumet, S. (Dir.) 1964. *The Pawnbroker* (Landau Company).
Minns, P. (Dir.) 2000. *The Hunger Business* (First Circle Films).

Pierson, F. (Dir.) 2001. *Conspiracy* (British Broadcasting Corporation, Home Box Office).

References

Adelman, H., A. Suhrke, and B. Jones. 1996. 'Chapter 4: Crisis and Withdrawal (6 April 1994– 21 April 1994)', in H. Adelman, A. Suhrke, and B. Jones (eds), *The International Response to Conflict and Genocide: Lessons from the Rwanda Experience. Study 2, Early Warning and Conflict Management*. Copenhagen: Joint Evaluation of Emergency Assistance to Rwanda, pp. 40–47.

Arendt, H. 1994[1963]. *Eichmann in Jerusalem: A Report on the Banality of Evil*, revised and enlarged ed. Harmondsworth: Penguin.

Ball, K. 2000. 'Trauma and Its Institutional Destinies', *Cultural Critique* 46(Autumn):1–44.

Barnett, M.N. 2002. *Eyewitness to a Genocide: The United Nations and Rwanda*. Ithaca: Cornell University Press.

British Film Institute. 2005a. *Special Preview: Shooting Dogs - Production Notes*. London: British Film Institute.

British Film Institute. 2005b. 'Interview with Michael Caton-Jones and John Hurt'. Retrieved 1 November from http://www.bfi.org.uk/features/interviews/caton-jones_hurt.html

Cargas, H.J. 1986. 'An Interview with Elie Wiesel', *Holocaust and Genocide Studies* 1(1): 5–10.

Chrétien, J.-P., Reporters sans frontières (Association), and UNESCO. 1995. *Rwanda, les médias du génocide*. Paris: Karthala.

Cowley, J. 2005. 'Rebirth of a Nation', *The Observer*, 27 February 2005. Retrieved 1 November 2011 from http://www.guardian.co.uk/film/2005/feb/27/features.review

Dallaire, R., and B. Beardsley. 2003. *Shake Hands with the Devil: The Failure of Humanity in Rwanda*. Toronto: Random House Canada.

Deme, A. 2006. 'Hotel Rwanda: Setting the Record Straight,' in *Counter Punch*. Retrieved 1 November 2011 from http://www.counterpunch.org/2006/04/24/hotel-rwanda/

Des Forges, A. 1999. *'Leave none to tell the story': Genocide in Rwanda*. New York; Paris: Human Rights Watch; International Federation of Human Rights.

Duage-Roth, A. 2010. *Writing and Filming the Genocide of the Tutsis in Rwanda: Dismembering and Remembering Traumatic History*. Lanham, MD: Lexington Books.

Eaglestone, R. 2001. *Postmodernism and Holocaust Denial*. Cambridge: Icon Books.

Eltringham, N. 2004. *Accounting for Horror: Post-Genocide Debates in Rwanda*. London: Pluto.
Errington, S. 1979. 'Some Comments on Style in the Meaning of the Past', *Journal of Asian Studies* 38(2):231–44.
Farrell, K. 1998. *Post-traumatic Culture: Injury and Interpretation in the Nineties*. Baltimore: Johns Hopkins University Press.
Fein, H. 1993. *Genocide: A Sociological Perspective*. London: Sage.
Feldman, A. 2000. 'Violence and Vision: The Prosthetics and Aesthetics of Terror', in V. Das (ed.), *Violence and Subjectivity*. Berkeley: University of California Press, pp. 46–78
———. 2004. 'Memory Theatres, Virtual Witnessing, and the Trauma-Aesthetic', *Biography* 27(1):163–202.
French, P. 2005. 'Schindler in Rwanda', *The Observer*, 27 February 2005. Retrieved 1 November 2011 from http://www.guardian.co.uk/film/2005/feb/27/philipfrench
Garfinkel, H. 1967. *Studies in Ethnomethodology*. Cambridge: Polity.
George, T. 2005. 'My Promise', in T. George (ed.), *Hotel Rwanda: Bringing the True Story of an African Hero to Film*. New York: Newmarket Press, pp. 33–45.
———. 2006. 'Smearing a Hero; Sad Revisionism Over "Hotel Rwanda"', in *Washington Post*, 10 May 2006. Retrieved 1 November from http://www.washingtonpost.com/wp-dyn/content/article/2006/05/09/AR2006050901242.html
Gouri, H. 2004. *Facing the Glass Booth: The Jerusalem Trial of Adolf Eichmann*. Detroit, MI: Wayne State University Press; London: Eurospan.
Gregory, S.A.M. 2006. 'Transnational Storytelling: Human Rights, WITNESS, and Video Advocacy', *American Anthropologist* 108(1):195–204.
Haidu, P. 1992. 'The Dialectics of Unspeakability: Language, Silence, and the Narratives of Desubjectification', in S. Friedländer (ed.), *Probing the Limits of Representation: Nazism and the "Final Solution"*. Cambridge, MA: Harvard University Press, pp. 277–99.
Halbwachs, M., and L.A. Coser. 1992. *On Collective Memory. The Heritage of Sociology*. Chicago: University of Chicago Press.
Hatzfeld, J. 2005. *Machete Season: The Killers in Rwanda Speak*. New York: Farrar, Straus and Giroux.
Hirsch, H. 1995. *Genocide and the Politics of Memory: Studying Death to Preserve Life*. Chapel Hill, London: University of North Carolina Press.
Hirsch, J.F. 2004. *Afterimage: Film, Trauma, and the Holocaust. Emerging Media*. Philadelphia: Temple University Press.
Hughes, N. 2007. 'Exhibit 467: Genocide through a Camera Lens', in A. Thompson (ed.), *The Media and the Rwanda Genocide*. London: Pluto, pp. 231–234.
Huyssen, A. 1980. 'The Politics of Identification: "Holocaust" and West German Drama', *New German Critique* 19(Winter):117–36.

Jackson, M. 2002. *The Politics of Storytelling: Violence, Transgression, and Intersubjectivity*. Copenhagen: Museum Tusculanum Press.
Jay, M. 1992. 'Of Plots, Witnesses, and Judgements', in S. Friedländer (ed.), *Probing the Limits of Representation: Nazism and the "Final Solution"*. Cambridge, MA: Harvard University Press, pp. 97–107.
Keane, F. 2006. 'Yes, we did cover horror of Rwanda', *The Observer*, 26 March 2006. Retrieved 1 November 2011 from http://www.guardian.co.uk/commentisfree/2006/mar/26/comment.television
Langer, L.L. 1997. 'The Alarmed Vision: Social Suffering and the Holocaust Atrocity', in A. Kleinman, V. Das and M.M. Lock (eds), *Social Suffering*. Berkeley: University of California Press, pp. 47–65.
Laub, D. 1992. 'Bearing Witness or the Vicissitudes of Listening', in S. Felman and D. Laub (eds), *Testimony: Crises of Witnessing in Literature, Psychoanalysis, and History*. New York; London: Routledge, pp. 57–74.
Levi, P. 1989. *The Drowned and the Saved*. London: Abacus.
Longman, T.P. 2009. *Christianity and Genocide in Rwanda*. Cambridge: Cambridge University Press.
Mackie, R. 2006. 'Review of Shooting Dogs', *The Guardian*, 4 August 2006. Retrieved 1 November 2011 from http://www.guardian.co.uk/film/2006/aug/04/dvdreviews.drama
Malkki, L.H. 1996. 'Speechless Emissaries: Refugees, Humanitarianism, and Dehistoricization', *Cultural Anthropology* 11(3):377–404.
Melvern, L. 2000. *A People Betrayed: The Role of the West in Rwanda's Genocide*. London: Zed Books.
Milmo, C. 2006. 'Flashback to terror: Survivors of Rwandan genocide watch screening of Shooting Dogs', *The Independent*, 29 March 2006. Retrieved 1 November 2011 from http://www.independent.co.uk/news/world/africa/flashback-to-terror-survivors-of-rwandan-genocide-watch-screening-of-shooting-dogs-471825.html
Mironko, C. 2006. '*Ibitero*: means and motive in Rwandan genocide', in S.E. Cook (ed.), *Genocide in Cambodia and Rwanda: New Perspectives*. New Brunswick, NJ: Transaction Publishers, pp. 173–99.
Mugabo, C. 2007. 'Paul Rusesabagina the self-declared saviour, treacherous liar', *The New Times*, Kigali, 25 May 2007.
Ndahiro, A., and P. Rutazibwa. 2008. *Hotel Rwanda, or, The Tutsi Genocide as Seen by Hollywood*. Paris: Harmattan.
Pearson, K. 2005. 'The Beginning', in T. George (ed.), *Hotel Rwanda: Bringing the True Story of an African Hero to Film*. New York: Newmarket Press, pp. 33–45
Rorty, R. 1998. 'Human Rights, Rationality and sentimentality', in R. Rorty (ed.), *Truth and Progress*. Cambridge: Cambridge University Press, pp. 111–134.
Roseman, M. 2003. *The Villa, the Lake, the Meeting: Wannsee and the Final Solution*. London and New York: Penguin Books.

Rosenstone, R.A. 1992. 'JFK: Historical Fact/Historical Film', *The American Historical Review* 97(2):506–511.

———. 2000. 'The Historical Film: Looking at the Past in a Postliterate Age'', in M. Landy (ed.), *The Historical Film: History and Memory in Media*. New Brunswick, NJ: Rutgers University Press, pp. 50–66.

Rusesabagina, P. 2006. 'Hero of Hotel Rwanda Calls Kagame a War Criminal', Retrieved 1 November 2011 from http://www.taylor-report.com/articles/index.php?id=28

Rusesabagina, P. and T. Zoellner. 2006. *An Ordinary Man*. London: Bloomsbury.

Santner, E.L. 1992. 'History beyond the Pleasure Principal: Some Thoughts on the Representation of Trauma', in S. Friedlander (ed.,) *Probing the Limits of Representation: Nazism and the Final Solution*'. Cambridge MA: Harvard University Press, pp. 143–54

Schaffer, K., and S. Smith. 2004. 'Conjunctions: Life Narratives in the Field of Human Rights', *Biography* 27(1):1–24.

Sontag, S. 2003. *Regarding the Pain of Others*. London: Penguin Books.

Straus, S. 2006. *The Order of Genocide: Race, Power, and War in Rwanda*. Ithaca, NY: Cornell University Press; Bristol: University Presses Marketing [distributor].

Toplin, R.B. 1996. *History by Hollywood: The Use and Abuse of the American Past*. Urbana: University of Illinois Press.

Torchin, L. 2006. 'Ravished Armenia: Visual Media, Humanitarian Advocacy, and the Formation of Witnessing Publics', *American Anthropologist* 108(1):214–20.

Waldorf, L. 2009. 'Revisiting "Hotel Rwanda": Genocide Ideology, Reconciliation, and Rescuers', *Journal of Genocide Research* 11(1):101–25.

Walker, R. 2004. 'Bringing Genocide to the Big Screen', *BBC News*, 2 August 2004. Retrieved 1 November 2011 from http://news.bbc.co.uk/1/hi/entertainment/3527130.stm

Walkowitz, D.J. 1985. 'Visual History: The Craft of the Historian-Filmmaker', *The Public Historian* 7(1):53–63.

Weiss, P., and A. Gross. 1966. *The Investigation*. London: Calder and Boyars.

Wiesel, E. 1978. 'Trivializing the Holocaust: Semi-Fact and Semi-Fiction', *The New York Times*, 16 April 1978, pp. 5–10.

Wrong, M. 2005. 'Horror movies', *The Guardian*, 18 February 2005. Retrieved 1 November 2011 from http://www.guardian.co.uk/film/2005/feb/18/2

Zur, J. 1997. 'Reconstructing the Self through Memories of Violence among Mayan Indian War Widows', in L. Ronit (ed.), *Gender and Catastrophe*. London: Zed, pp. 64–76.

Six

Torture, Betrayal and Forgiveness
Red Dust and the Search for Truth in Post-Apartheid South Africa

Annelies Verdoolaege

Introduction

The landscape looks reddish and dusty at the onset of the film *Red Dust* (2004). Immediately we witness a convoy of large trucks thundering through the barren interior of South Africa, the symbol of the Truth and Reconciliation Commission painted on their sides; it is 2000 and the itinerant Commission is coming to town. The town referred to is Smitsrivier, a fictional town where the nightmares that took place under the apartheid regime are about to be relived.

The South African Truth and Reconciliation Commission (TRC) was a unique conflict-resolving mechanism, where amnesty was granted in exchange for the truth.[1] It is the proceedings of the TRC, and more specifically of the Amnesty Committee of the TRC, that is the dominant storyline of this film. Being a multilayered film, though, this dominant storyline is intertwined with a number of other storylines: the narratives of betrayal, companionship, forgiveness and – however marginal – love. *Red Dust* is not an easy film to watch. From the first bloody frames a number of scenes are disturbing, gruesome and emotionally difficult to deal with, especially the scenes of torture and the exhumation of the remains of the murdered Umkhonto we Sizwe (armed wing of the African National Congress) comrade. In addition, restorative justice and its challenging principles of amnesty, reconciliation and forgiveness are not mainstream topics and one can speculate that an audience unfamiliar with these principles may find it hard to follow.

In this chapter I will explore whether or not *Red Dust* gives a truthful portrayal of the proceedings of the South African TRC. I will do this by referring to key issues that are addressed in the film, including torture, betrayal and forgiveness. First, however, I will give an overview of the context in which the TRC emerged and the objectives it was designed to fulfil.

The South African Truth and Reconciliation Commission – A Unique Principle

As the South African TRC was an attempt to deal with the atrocities committed under apartheid, it is important to first give some general background information on the apartheid regime. Apartheid can be described as 'the social and political policy of racial segregation and discrimination enforced by white minority governments in South Africa from 1948–1994' (Appiah and Gates 1999: 118). The term was first recorded in 1917, during a speech by Jan Smuts, who became Prime Minister of South Africa in 1919. In Afrikaans the word means 'separation' or literally *aparthood* (or 'apartness'). Apartheid was an institutionalized form of racial discrimination, officialising different rights and obligations for different racial groups in South Africa, and it came into being after the National Party (NP) won the general elections in 1948. A distinction is generally made between 'grand apartheid' and 'petty apartheid': 'grand apartheid' was centred on separating races on a large scale, by compelling people to live in separate places defined by race. This led to the creation of the so-called *Bantustans* or 'homelands', where black South Africans had to live together on the basis of ethnicity and where they became nothing more than cheap labour force for the booming South African mining industry. In addition 'petty apartheid' laws were passed, such as the Prohibition of Mixed Marriages Act (1949), prohibiting marriage between persons of different races, or the Bantu Education Act (1953), which designed a separate system of education for African students – mainly focusing on vocational training (Verdoolaege and Van Keymeulen 2010: 14). Between 1960 and 1983 the apartheid government forcibly removed over 3.5 million black South Africans. In addition, as a result of the internal opposition against apartheid and the increasing militarization of the South African state, numerous gross human rights violations were committed (such as murder, torture, rape, arson, abduction). Towards the end of the 1980s a few petty laws were repealed and following growing internal resistance (with anti-apartheid movements such as the African National Congress (ANC) or the Pan Africanist Congress (PAC)) and international opposition, it became clear that in the long run apartheid would not be a viable solution for South Africa. Formal negotiations between the ANC and the NP took place in the first half of the 1990s, after the release of ANC leader Nelson Mandela, and apartheid officially came to an end with the national elections on 27 April 1994.

After the demise of apartheid in 1994 the South African government (see Catsam, this volume) was confronted with the need to deal with the atrocities that had happened in the past. After long negotiations, where especially the ANC and the NP discussed the possibilities available to confront the past, a decision was made to set up a truth commission. The idea of a truth commission for South Africa first came from the ANC. As soon as it was legalized in February 1990, accusations were launched against the party that it had committed human rights violations in some of its training camps in Tanzania and in other southern African countries. The response of the ANC was to set up its own internal investigation commissions, amongst others the Stuart, the Skweyiya and the Motsuenyane commissions. These commissions confirmed that gross human rights violations had taken place in the camps during the time of exile, findings that were accepted by the National Executive Committee (NEC) of the ANC. However, in response to the Motsuenyane Commission's report, the NEC did call upon the government to 'set up, without delay, a Commission of Inquiry or Truth Commission into all violations of human rights since 1948' (Boraine 2000: 12).

The South African Truth and Reconciliation Commission was called into existence in July 1995. The Preamble of the Promotion of National Unity and Reconciliation Act No. 34 of 1995 (the TRC Act)[2] stated that the objectives of the TRC were to promote national unity and reconciliation by establishing as complete a picture as possible of the gross violations of human rights which were committed under apartheid, by facilitating the granting of amnesty to apartheid perpetrators under certain conditions, and by providing recommendations to prevent future violations of human rights (TRC Report 1998, 1/4: 54).[3] In order to achieve its ambitious objectives, three subcommittees of the TRC were put into place: the Committee for Human Rights Violations, the Amnesty Committee and the Reparation and Rehabilitation Committee.

The Human Rights Violations Committee is generally considered as the most successful of the three TRC committees. This committee invited victims of human rights abuses to make statements about their suffering in the past. More than 21,000 people came forward to talk about their experiences under apartheid, a response greater than any previous truth commission. About 10 per cent of these victims were then invited to tell their stories in public. The public hearings started on 15 April 1996 and they lasted for about two years. This committee, therefore, provided a platform for thousands of victims to talk about their experiences, allowing a great deal of truth about the past to be revealed.

The aim of the Amnesty Committee (AC) – which is the component of the TRC that takes central position in *Red Dust* – was to grant amnesty to apartheid perpetrators, although only under a number of strict conditions: the crime had to be committed between 1 May 1960 and 10 May 1994, there had to be a political motive and the perpetrator had to disclose the full truth about the crime. The Amnesty Committee also organized public hearings, but with insufficient time, not all of the amnesty applications could be dealt with in this way. Applications were divided into three groups: 'hearable matters' (those applications involving gross human rights violations and requiring a public hearing); 'chamber matters' (applications involving violations of human rights which were not 'gross' as defined by the Act and which did not require a public hearing – they were considered by the AC in chambers); and 'possible refusals' (applications that, at least superficially, did not qualify for amnesty in terms of the Act – these applications first had to be corroborated by the Investigation Unit) (TRC Report 1998, 1/10: 269; Eyskens 2001: 31; Wilson 2001: 23). Although the Amnesty Committee received a little over 7,100 applications, the vast majority were turned down. The granting of amnesty was controversial, as it acquitted perpetrators of any further legal or civil prosecution. The TRC claimed, though, that without this provision of amnesty, the perpetrators would never have come forward and they would never have revealed the truth about their crimes (Boraine 2000: 23; Eyskens 2001: 38).

The third, and final, committee of the TRC was the Committee on Reparation and Rehabilitation. Its main task was to evaluate the statements and applications provided by the Human Rights Violations Committee and the Amnesty Committee. Based on this material, the committee had to formulate recommendations regarding the compensation of victims.

While an interim report of the TRC's findings was presented to President Mandela in October 1998, the proceedings of the Amnesty Committee continued well into 2001 because of the large number of amnesty applications. The Final Report of the TRC was not released until March 2003.

The fact that the Commission did not really have the authority to implement the recommendations of the Committee on Reparation and Rehabilitation is often seen as one of the major shortcomings of the TRC. In addition, a lot of questions have been asked with regard to the long-term effects of the Commission. During the proceedings of the TRC the Commission was generally praised a lot, inside South Africa as well as abroad. People particularly seemed to welcome the fact that a great deal of truth was revealed at the victim hearings (Chapman 2008). Once the TRC drew to a close, however, doubts were raised regarding the value of the whole process. It was argued that the Commission had been worthwhile for the victims who had testified, but that the majority of apartheid survivors did not benefit at all (Stanley 2001). Instead, the apartheid perpetrators were seen as the main beneficiaries. Some of them came forward and were humiliated in public, but the majority just ran the risk of keeping quiet. The idea of the TRC process was that perpetrators who did not come forward would be prosecuted, but in reality the government did not pursue prosecutions (Graybill 2002: 74). Many South Africans also claimed that the TRC had not really worked towards a more positive attitude between black and white. Racial tension and material inequality did not seem to have changed drastically since 1994, so many people were not at all convinced the TRC had been valuable (Daly and Sarkin 2007).

It is now commonly agreed that the mandate of the TRC was too ambitious. The aspirations of revealing the truth, striving for reconciliation, listening to the victims of apartheid, and granting amnesty to the perpetrators, were each very difficult to realize. Only a fraction of the atrocities that took place under apartheid were revealed, not all of the victims came forward, high-ranking apartheid officials did not apply for amnesty, and the TRC could do nothing more than start a process of reconciliation. South Africa today is, however, a relatively peaceful and democratic society (Verdoolaege 2008); advocates for the TRC claim that this stable situation is a result of the Commission and that the real effects of its work will only be visible after some more years. The TRC is often considered as a model for what is termed 'restorative justice' (Llewellyn and Howse 1999; van Zyl 1999; Villa-Vicencio 2000). Restorative justice is about restoring victims, offenders and communities and according to some scholars it is an ideal way to address issues of justice in transitional contexts. The TRC has indeed been taken as an example in many post-traumatic conflict situations[4] and the staff of the South African TRC have been travelling the world to talk about their experiences. It cannot be denied that the TRC has not only changed the history of South Africa, but that it also had a global impact on mechanisms of conflict resolution.

It is against this background that one could (or maybe should) understand the film *Red Dust*. In what follows I will first give a short synopsis of the film and then elaborate on three key themes.

The TRC in Smitsrivier

The setting of *Red Dust* is a very important feature of the film. Although fictional, the town of Smitsrivier is an iconic conservative town in the interior of South Africa. These were the towns where young 'black lions' of the ANC stood up against racial oppression, where white policemen were lord and master and where white girls were arrested when dating a black boyfriend. These were also the towns where apartheid continued in the post-1994 era. In everyday life apartheid is still clearly visible in those towns – people from various population groups tend to frequent different bars and shops, mixed relationships are rare and white policemen are still held in high esteem.

In this dusty town of Smitsrivier we witness the arrival of Sarah Barcant (Hilary Swank), an NYC lawyer who grew up in South Africa. She has been called back to her home town by Ben Hoffman (Marius Weyers), a white lawyer who has fought all of his life against apartheid and who is a fervent proponent of the principle of restorative justice. Sarah Barcant can be seen as his protégé, for it is Hoffman who got her out of prison when she was arrested for having a black boyfriend when she was sixteen. Barcant wants to do Hoffman a favour by defending Alex Mpondo (Chiwetel Ejiofor), a black ANC politician who was tortured under apartheid in 1986. His torturer, local policeman Dirk Hendricks (Jamie Bartlett), applies for amnesty before the TRC and Mpondo is determined to appeal against this amnesty application. In the course of the amnesty hearing, it appears that under severe torture Mpondo identified one of his underground comrades, Steve Sizela (Loyiso Gxwala), who was subsequently killed in prison. Gradually, the whole truth is revealed: Hendricks admits that Sizela was in fact killed by his boss, Pieter Muller (Ian Roberts), and testifies to the existence of a 'torture farm' in the vicinity of Smitsrivier; and he tells Mpondo that his friend Sizela is buried close to that farm. Eventually, the bones of Steve Sizela are found, much to the relief of Sizela's parents, and Mpondo decides to allow amnesty for Hendricks, as the whole truth has been said. Muller, charged with the murder of Sizela, then also applies for amnesty.

This synopsis tells us that *Red Dust* could be enjoyed as an entertaining film by non-experts. However, is seems unlikely that non-experts would be able to understand the wider context, the links with apartheid history and – in particular – the impact the TRC exerted on post-apartheid South Africa. I shall now explore three key themes of the film. By contextualising these themes, I will then assess the film's veracity.

Torture

The theme of torture is prevalent in *Red Dust,* in particular because of the vivid scenes in which torture practices are shown – especially the torture of Alex Mpondo, but also of his comrade Steve Sizela. One of the objectives of the TRC was to 'designate accountability for gross human rights violations' (TRC Report 1998, 1/10: 267) and according to the TRC Act 'gross violation of human rights' referred to the 'violation of human rights through the killing, abduction, torture or severe ill-treatment of any person' (TRC Act, article ix). Torture was one of the politically motivated gross violations of human rights for which apartheid perpetrators could ask amnesty.

The extent to which torture was practised by security forces under apartheid was strikingly revealed during the human rights violations hearings of the TRC – the hearings where the victims of apartheid violations came forward to tell their stories. Many of these survivors described in great detail how they were abused or tortured and because of the public nature of these hearings these torture practices became common knowledge in South Africa and beyond. At the Amnesty Committee, however, amnesty applications for torture were 'extraordinarily limited in number when compared to the vast numbers of cases of torture reported to the TRC by victims' (Fullard and Rousseau 2003: 212). According to Fullard and Rousseau, this may be due to the 'unprovable' and private nature of torture. Given that full disclosure of what had happened during apartheid was required to be granted amnesty, many amnesty applicants admitted that they had abused prisoners while interrogating them. Many times, however, the discourse used by the perpetrators was veiled and it tended to be much vaguer than the descriptions of brutal and extensive torture given by the victims. Perpetrators applying for amnesty often used general terms like 'assaulting', 'hitting', 'punching' or 'kicking', without mentioning what they did concretely. This is illustrated in the film where Hendricks describes having a 'conversation' with Mpondo while a flashback shows police beating him. Also, as noted by Fullard and Rousseau (2003: 212), perpetrators would rarely admit 'any form of torture that involved the genitals or sexual organs in any way', while surviving victims often testified to electroshocks or burns on the genitals.

Amnesty applicants generally took a very distant attitude towards the horrible facts they were recounting. They repeatedly stressed that they could not remember what exactly had happened, especially with regard to torture or (sexual) abuse. They often claimed that they had lost memory as a result of Post-Traumatic Stress Disorder (PTSD), an anxiety disorder that can develop after the experience of a psychological trauma. This is clearly illustrated in the film, as we often notice how Hendricks tells his story with a face void of emotions, while emphasizing continuously how he cannot recall what exactly happened to the ANC comrades in prison. Hendricks also claims to be suffering from PTSD, and in this way he manages to picture himself as a victim instead of a perpetrator. This must have been extremely hard for victims to bear; this is illustrated in a scene in which, during the TRC hearing, Hendricks claims that 'the doctor said I had suffered PTSD' at which Mpondo jumps off the stage and storms out of the packed hall.

Some amnesty applicants did describe their torture methods in great detail, but these were exceptions. One notorious example of an amnesty applicant who demonstrated which techniques he used in order to get information from the liberation fighters was Jeffrey Benzien (see Krog 1998: 109–17). His demonstration of the 'wet bag' method at the public amnesty hearing in July 1997 has been widely publicized. When asked by Tony Yengeni, former ANC activist who had been tortured by Benzien himself, Benzien demonstrates the wet bag method by making use of a volunteer. The method involved a bag soaked in water, which was pulled over the head of the victim and twisted tightly around his neck, cutting off the air supply to the victim. The suspect was then questioned. From time to time the bag was released to avoid the victim losing consciousness. As testified by Benzien, this self-designed technique was so effective that he always got the desired results within thirty minutes.[5]

Benzien's demonstration makes for one of the most dramatic and also one of the most sensationalised instances of the TRC hearings. It is clear that the makers of *Red Dust* are referring to this torture method when Dirk Hendricks finally admits that he has been torturing his victims. In what follows we see how Mpondo is being tortured by means of a wet bag and we hear Hendricks claiming how this method could be applied over and over again, until the victim broke down. In the film the torture technique is not demonstrated by the amnesty applicant, but by inserting images of the torturing of Mpondo, the viewer gets a very vivid description of what the method was about.

It is clear that with regard to torture – and also regarding the stern attitude of the amnesty applicants, *Red Dust* is very faithful to the original TRC hearings. In the scenes of the hearing itself, it seems as if the viewer is actually experiencing a TRC amnesty hearing, witnessing the anxiety and frustration of the victim, and the cold-bloodedness of the perpetrator.

Betrayal

While testifying before the TRC, Dirk Hendricks claims that Alex Mpondo, after severe torture, identified his friend Steve Sizela as a fellow comrade in the struggle – following which the latter was killed in prison. This revelation comes as a huge shock to Mpondo, who keeps telling himself (and other ex-liberation fighters) that he never broke under torture. The public announcement by Hendricks – in front of Steve Sizela's parents – is emotionally almost too much for Mpondo.

At the beginning of the film one sees Mpondo being welcomed by his friends upon his arrival in the township. He is identified as a hero who struggled for liberation and who became a successful politician after the 1994 transition. This positive image is drastically altered after the revelation by Hendricks: Mpondo is then openly insulted and accused of being a traitor, his bravery is gone and he is convinced this will be the end of his political career. This is clearly a very difficult moment for Alex Mpondo. It is indicated that over the last couple of years he has been struggling with his own consciousness about the question of whether or not he 'betrayed' his friend Sizela. He has finally come to the conclusion that he never gave in, and it is a position he maintains at the TRC hearings. After Hendricks' testimony, however, everybody seems to be convinced that Mpondo did indeed break under torture. This is a great blow for the Sizela parents, who now hear that their son was actually betrayed by one of his fellow comrades. At this moment in the film the story has reached rock-bottom, especially because of the way in which the formerly revered Alex Mpondo is now treated as a criminal.

Betraying a fellow comrade after being tortured in prison was indeed a highly sensitive issue under apartheid. Some of the survivors testifying before the Human Rights Violations Committee did speak about the way they were tortured, and how this distress sometimes made them accuse or identify other freedom fighters. Often, it was not only their personal torture, but also the threat of what the police would do to loved ones that caused them to break. Yazir Henry, for example, during his testimony before the Human Rights Violation Committee (on 6 August 1996) told the audience how he had led the police to his fellow comrade Anton Fransch, after severe interrogation (see Henry 2000: 166–73; Krog 1998: 79–83). This testimony of Yazir Henry is horrifying, as Henry psychologically breaks down while testifying. Later on Henry explains how he was called names and even insulted as a result of his testimony before the TRC. Freedom fighters were not supposed to collaborate with the police, not even under torture – if they did, they could be labelled an *askari* [6] or they could be 'necklaced'.[7]

These episodes of the film, where the agony of Alex Mpondo is clearly illustrated, are truthful to what actually went on in cases where betrayal was revealed at the hearings of the TRC. At the amnesty hearing of Jeffrey Benzien – on which Hendricks' fictional testimony clearly seems to be modelled – Benzien addresses the victim after having demonstrated the wet bag method, and he reminds him of the fact that he broke under torture and subsequently betrayed a fellow comrade. The parallels with *Red Dust* are striking, as we understand from this extract from Krog (1998: 110):

> Back at the table, Benzien quietly turns on him and with one accurate blow shatters Yengeni's political profile right across the country.
>
> 'Do you remember, Mr. Yengeni, that within thirty minutes you betrayed Jennifer Schreiner? Do you remember pointing out Bongani Jonas to us on the highway?'

The same code of honour also existed amongst the members of the security forces. In the beginning of *Red Dust* we see how Dirk Hendricks meets Pieter Muller, Smitsrivier's former police boss – this happens in unclear circumstances, probably at the time when Hendricks is being transported to the venue where the amnesty hearings will take place. Muller does not object to Hendricks' application for amnesty, but he wants to make sure Hendricks will not mention his name, despite the fact that one of the criteria to be granted amnesty is to tell the whole truth. For most of the film Hendricks is indecisive as to whether he should remain loyal to Muller, or tell the whole truth. Muller is actually the police officer who interrogated and tortured Steve Sizela to death; as a proud and authoritative former policeman he does not want to apply for amnesty. And indeed, in Dirk Hendricks' amnesty hearing it is only the case of Alex Mpondo that is being considered. It is only gradually, in the course of the hearing, that the two cases (Mpondo and Sizela) become connected when Hendricks claims that Mpondo betrayed his friend. The parents of Steve Sizela, present at the hearing, hope that this will be an opportunity to reveal the truth about what happened to their son, but the judge leading the hearing formally announces that only the case of Alex Mpondo should be referred to at this hearing. It is only at the end of the film that Muller will be implicated – for he also applies for amnesty. The twist is that the audience finally discovers that although Muller killed Sizela, it was Hendricks who buried the body and with it the charge sheet that would implicate Muller.

Over a time-span of almost two years (from December 1995 to 30 September 1997, which was the final date for the submission of applications) the Amnesty Committee received 7,112 applications (TRC Report 1998, 1/10: 266). In the first phase only a few people applied for amnesty at the Amnesty Committee, but as time went by more apartheid perpetrators came to ask for pardon. Especially after some heavyweight members of the security forces and the liberation movements had come forward, the number of amnesty applicants increased – mostly because people were implicated in earlier applications and were afraid of prosecution if they were not going to appear before the TRC (Boraine 2000: 122). In the final two months before the deadline about 1,000 people applied.

This phenomenon is exactly what we witness in the film *Red Dust*: in many cases – notwithstanding a few noteworthy exceptions – apartheid perpetrators only applied for amnesty when they were already convicted and serving sentences (and hoped to be released on the basis of their testimony), or when their name was

147

mentioned in the amnesty application of someone else. This reveals one of the shortcomings of the TRC mechanism. When bearing in mind how ruthless apartheid was executed in every little village in South Africa, and how many people were killed, tortured or abused, the number of 7,112 amnesty applications is very low. Many perpetrators knew that, most likely, they were not going to be prosecuted if they did not apply for amnesty. Up until today only very few apartheid perpetrators who did not come forward to the TRC, have been brought to court – which is generally seen as one of the main problems in post-TRC South Africa. It has been argued that, had there been a parallel criminal process alongside the TRC, many more perpetrators would have come forward to tell the truth about the apartheid atrocities. That the TRC did not grant blanket amnesty was very laudable, but the threat of court cases might have yielded even bigger results (Sarkin 2008: 115).

Forgiveness

After the film has reached rock-bottom and Alex Mpondo has fallen from his pedestal, we witness a turning point in the storyline of *Red Dust*. All of a sudden, Mpondo remembers that he was not tortured in the police station of Smitsrivier, but rather in a farm-like building. Hendricks then confesses that he used to bring his suspects to a farm outside Smitsrivier, where they were interrogated. He also admits that he buried the body of Steve Sizela in the vicinity of that farm.

A farm as a location where members of the anti-apartheid movements were interrogated and killed figured prominently in testimonies before the TRC. The farm mostly referred to is Vlakplaas, a farm twenty kilometres west of Pretoria that served as the headquarters of the counter-insurgency group of the South African Police. This group was commanded by Eugene de Kock and it was well known for killing, torturing and murdering hundreds of anti-apartheid activists. Eugene de Kock applied for amnesty at the TRC, as a result of which he was named Prime Evil by the media. The resemblance between Vlakplaas and the farm that features in *Red Dust* is striking.

While they are both at the farm Hendricks tells Alex Mpondo where he buried the body of Steve Sizela, whereupon we witness the exhumation of Sizela's remains. The exhumation of human remains was part of the mandate given to the TRC. The Commission was to 'establish the whereabouts of those who had disappeared' and the Investigation Unit of the TRC investigated many cases of reported disappearances. After investigation many secret burial sites were exposed or identified by perpetrators (TRC Report 1998, 2/6: 534). Fifty bodies were exhumed by the TRC, but almost 200 cases were not finalized – 'because of the lengthy procedure necessitated by each exhumation' (TRC Report 1998, 2/6: 534). The scenes in *Red Dust* showing how the bones of Steve Sizela are found, how he is identified by means of a necklace and how Steve's mother (Nomhlé Nkyonyeni) starts crying and throws herself upon the grave, are very similar to the internationally broadcast images of exhumations carried out by the TRC – the family members were usually present, indeed, and the women, especially, showed their grief, but also their relief because they had finally found the bones of their loved ones. In reality exhumations were never carried out at Vlakplaas, but as a consequence of Eugene de Kock's testimony before the Amnesty Committee, the secret burial places of a number of anti-apartheid activists were found.

As a result of Hendricks' willingness to reveal the burial place of Sizela, Alex Mpondo decides no longer to object to his torturer's amnesty application. This is the first layer of forgiveness the viewer witnesses. The second layer is when the parents of Sizela explicitly forgive Alex Mpondo for the death of their son. These instances of forgiveness come at the end of the film and that is where the viewer is confronted with the core of what the TRC was intended to be. One of the main objectives of the Truth and Reconciliation Commission was to bring victims and perpetrators closer to each other, to induce them to listen to each other and to respect one another – and, as a final aim, starting a process of national reconciliation (Mxolisi 2000; Villa-Vicencio 2000). Personal forgiveness did take place as a result of the TRC proceedings – or even at the TRC hearings themselves (such as the amnesty hearing where Ginn Fourie offered to forgive the members of the Azanian People's Liberation Army (APLA) who were responsible for the death of her daughter; or the hearing where the applicants responsible for the attack on the St James church – leaving eleven people dead and sixty wounded – shook hands with seventeen of the victims) (Tutu 1999: 120). Clearly, this personal forgiveness is touched upon in *Red Dust*, but the fact that personal forgiveness was not always self-evident, especially not vis-à-vis the torturer and murderer of one's child, is also illustrated at the very end of the film, where the parents of Steve Sizela are outraged about Pieter Muller's plan to apply for amnesty for the murder of their son. In this way the filmmakers attend to the ambivalent attitude to amnesty of many people in post-apartheid South Africa: while it could deliver a loved one's remains it could equally allow a murderer to go free.

The whole issue of national reconciliation, and the role the TRC played in this process, is expressed by Ben Hoffman, the lawyer who convinces Sarah Barcant to return to her homeland to defend Alex Mpondo before the TRC. Hoffman is very much in favour of the TRC process and he tries to explain to Barcant why the TRC is crucial for the future of South Africa. This is a very important moment in the film, as it gives the viewer the opportunity to understand the bigger picture of the whole TRC process: the TRC hearings were about revealing the truth, understanding one another and possibly trying to forgive one another, but they were also – and more importantly – about creating a unified and reconciled nation where people are willing to work together to build a new future. It is an entirely different debate whether or not these aspirations have been realized (see Borer 2006; du Bois and du Bois-Pedain 2008; Chapman and van der Merwe 2008), but it is clear that the makers of *Red Dust* have tried their best to touch upon the heart of the TRC endeavour – forgiveness and reconciliation on an interpersonal and national scale. As explained later on, though, this theme does not seem to be developed to the same extent as the two other (more sensational) topics discussed: torture and betrayal.

Discussion

Red Dust is an exciting and, at times, gripping film which manages to bring the complex mechanism of the South African Truth and Reconciliation Commission to a wider public. Let me, by summarizing the main topics discussed above, express some concluding comments.

As is clear from the larger context I gave above, the makers of *Red Dust* tried to be truthful to the original TRC proceedings. In particular, when viewing the film I appreciated the attention that was paid to certain details – details which seem insignificant, but which were very important for some of the participants in the TRC process. One of these 'details' – prominent in the first half of the film – has to do with the controversy around the word 'victim'. The term 'victim' was generally used by the TRC ('victim hearings', 'victim findings'), but a number of the so-called victims soon objected to the term. They wanted to be called 'survivors', as this term refers to the active role they had played in the liberation struggle – much more than the passive term 'victim'. Explicit attention is paid to this controversy in the film when Alex Mpondo throws away the cardboard sign saying 'victim' when he first takes his seat at the hearing and later on, when he refuses to be addressed as 'the victim' by Hendricks' lawyer. Another important detail is the reference to Post-Traumatic Stress Disorder and the fact that perpetrators tried their best to reverse the roles: depicting the 'victim' as the criminal who was waging a war against the state and portraying themselves as the victim who is traumatized and who has lost many friends as a result of what he did in the past. Finally, gender roles also take a prominent position in this film. As has been expressed by a number of critics (see Ross 2003; Krog 1998: 269), women were often secondary victims at the TRC – they testified about the killing, torture and disappearance of their sons, husbands and brothers, but they seldom talked about the hardship (abuse, rape) they had endured. The TRC was aware of these skewed gender roles and the Commission decided to organize special women's

151

hearings (taking place in Johannesburg, from 28 to 29 July 1997). Except for Sarah Barcant, it is the mother of Steve Sizela who is shown as a particularly strong woman in *Red Dust*. She is the one who is prepared to talk to Alex Mpondo – and who ultimately wants to forgive him – and she is also the one who takes a leading position when present at the hearings and at the exhumation of her son's remains.

The film *Red Dust* is of course an adaptation of the novel *Red Dust* (2000) by Gillian Slovo. The novel, so also the film, is highly autobiographical, as Gillian Slovo is the daughter of two anti-apartheid activists, Joe Slovo and Ruth First. At the amnesty hearings of the TRC she faced the murderer of her mother, an experience that was liberating to her, as she explained in a later interview. The fact that Slovo was closely connected to the struggle and the TRC process in South Africa is probably one of the reasons why the film has tried to stay truthful to reality – taking into account the details to which I have referred.

One could say, indeed, that *Red Dust* is a truthful reflection of the TRC process – especially with regard to the amnesty hearings. However, *Red Dust* is not a documentary; it is a British, commercial film, aimed at the general public. Therefore, a number of spectacular and media-friendly aspects of the TRC proceedings have been combined in this film. The character of Dirk Hendricks, for instance, symbolizes a number of notorious amnesty applicants, notably Jeffrey Benzien – the testifier who demonstrated the 'wet bag' torture method – and Eugene de Kock – the commander of Vlakplaas who was labelled Prime Evil, but who, as a result of his testimony, urged other apartheid perpetrators to come forward. Of the three themes discussed above, torture and betrayal are especially prominent in the film – two topics that lend themselves perfectly for a drama film. The third theme, which is definitely the most important when trying to understand the wider significance of the TRC, is present in a more subtle and less explicit manner. It is a theme that only reveals itself to the viewer who tries to look for the messages hidden behind the façade of the film.

Red Dust is a laudable film, in that it tries to shed light on a unique conflict-resolving mechanism. It is likely, though, that non-experts will see this film as simply a courtroom drama; many viewers would not understand the whole principle of 'truth in exchange for justice', that lay at the basis of the amnesty procedure. With a bit more contextual information – which could be given in one of the dialogues between Ben Hoffman and Sarah Barcant, or between Barcant and Alex Mpondo – the wider significance of the truth and reconciliation commission could have been presented more thoroughly. While the film does demonstrate what a tremendous impact the proceedings of the TRC had on the personal lives of some of its participants, it does not reflect sufficiently on what the TRC meant for the post-apartheid nation of South Africa.

Notes

1. Website of the Truth and Reconciliation Commission http://www.justice.gov.za/trc/
2. The text of the TRC act is available at http://www.justice.gov.za/legislation/acts/1995-034.pdf
3. The full reports are available at http://www.justice.gov.za/trc/report/index.htm
4. See http://ictj.org/
5. See http://www.justice.gov.za/trc/decisions/1999/99_benzien.htm
6. *Askari* is a Swahili word for soldiers or policemen. In South Africa it denoted former ANC members who had been forced to work for the South African Police (de Kock 1998: 305).
7. 'Necklacing' is a method of lethal lynching, whereby a tyre filled with petrol is set on fire around the victim's neck. In apartheid South Africa some supporters of the ANC applied this to persons alleged to be traitors of the liberation movement. The ANC has always officially condemned the practice (see Human Rights Watch Report 2008: http://www.hrw.org/reports/1991/southafrica1/6.htm).

Filmography

Hooper, T. (Dir.) 2004. *Red Dust* (British Broadcasting Corporation, Distant Horizon,
Videovision Entertainment, Industrial Development Corporation of South Africa, BBC Films).

References

Appiah, K.A. and H.L. Gates (eds). 1999. *Africana.* New York: Basic Civitas Books.

Bois du, F. and A. du Bois-Pedain (eds). 2008. *Justice and Reconciliation in Post-Apartheid South Africa.* Cambridge: Cambridge University Press.

Boraine, A. 2000. *A Country Unmasked. Inside South Africa's Truth and Reconciliation Commission.* Cape Town: Oxford University Press.

Borer, T.A. (ed.). 2006. *Telling the Truths. Truth Telling and Peace Building in Post-Conflict Societies.* Notre Dame: University of Notre Dame Press.

Chapman, A.R. 2008. 'The TRC's Approach to Promoting Reconciliation in the Human Rights Violations Hearings', in A.R. Chapman and H. van der Merwe (eds). *Truth and Reconciliation in South Africa: Did the TRC Deliver?* Philadelphia: University of Pennsylvania Press, pp. 45–65.

Chapman, A.R. and H. van der Merwe (eds). 2008. *Truth and Reconciliation in South Africa: Did the TRC Deliver?* Philadelphia: University of Pennsylvania Press.

Daly, E. and Sarkin, J. 2007. *Reconciliation in Divided Societies. Finding Common Ground.* Philadelphia: University of Pennsylvania Press.

Eyskens, L. 2001. 'Controverses over de Zuid-Afrikaanse Waarheids- en Verzoeningscommissie', M.A thesis. Ghent: Ghent University.

Fullard, M. and N. Rousseau. 2003. 'Truth, Evidence, and History: A Critical Review of Aspects of the Amnesty Process', in C. Villa-Vicencio and E. Doxtader (eds), *The Provocations of Amnesty: Memory, Justice and Impunity.* Claremont: David Philip Publishers, pp. 195–216.

Graybill, L.S. 2002. *Truth and Reconciliation in South Africa. Miracle or Model?* Boulder: Lynne Rienner Publishers, Inc.

Henry, Y. 2000. 'Where healing begins', in C. Villa-Vicencio and W. Verwoerd (eds), *Looking Back, Reaching Forward, Reflections on the Truth and Reconciliation Commission of South Africa.* Cape Town: University of Cape Town Press, pp. 166–73.

Kock de, E. 1998. *A Long Night's Damage: Working for the Apartheid State.* Saxonwold: Contra Press.

Krog, A. 1998. *Country of My Skull: Guilt, Sorrow, and the Limits of Forgiveness in the New South Africa.* Parklands: Random House South Africa.

Llewellyn, J.J. and R. Howse. 1999. 'Institutions for Restorative Justice: The South African Truth and Reconciliation Commission', *University of Toronto Law Journal* 49(3): 355–88.

Mxolisi, M. 2000. 'Reconciliation: a call to action', in C. Villa-Vicencio and W. Verwoerd (eds), *Looking Back, Reaching Forward: Reflections on the Truth and Reconciliation Commission of South Africa.* Cape Town: University of Cape Town Press, pp. 210–18.

Ross, F.C. 2003. *Bearing Witness: Women and the Truth and Reconciliation Commission in South Africa.* London: Pluto Press.

Sarkin, J. 2008. 'An Evaluation of the South African Amnesty Process', in A.R. Chapman and Hugo van der Merwe (eds), *Truth and Reconciliation in South Africa: Did the TRC Deliver?* Philadelphia: University of Pennsylvania Press, pp. 93–115.

Slovo, G. 2001. *Red Dust.* Kettering: Virago.

Stanley, E. 2001. 'Identities, Truth and Reconciliation in South Africa: Some International Concerns', in P. Kennedy and C.J. Danks (eds), *Globalisation, National Identities. Crisis or Opportunity.* Houndmills: Palgrave, pp. 175–89.

Tutu, D.1999. *No Future without Forgiveness: A Personal Overview of South Africa's Truth and Reconciliation Commission.* London: Rider Books.

Verdoolaege, A. 2008. *Reconciliation Discourse. The Case of the Truth and Reconciliation Commission.* Amsterdam: John Benjamins Publishing Company.

Verdoolaege, A and J. Van Keymeulen. 2010. *Grammatica van het Afrikaans.* Ghent: Academia Press.

Villa-Vicencio, C. 2000. 'Restorative justice: dealing with the past differently', in C. Villa-Vicencio and W. Verwoerd (eds), *Looking Back, Reaching Forward: Reflections on the Truth and Reconciliation Commission of South Africa.* Cape Town: University of Cape Town Press, pp. 68–76.

Wilson, R.A. 2001. *The Politics of Truth and Reconciliation in South Africa. Legitimising the Post-Apartheid State.* Cambridge: Cambridge University Press.

Zyl van, P. 1999. 'Dilemmas of transitional justice: the case of South Africa's Truth and Reconciliation Commission', *Journal of International Affairs* 52(2): 648–64.

Seven

Go *Amabokoboko!* Rugby, Race, Madiba and the *Invictus* Creation Myth of a New South Africa

Derek Charles Catsam

Nelson Mandela, Ubuntu and the Springboks

The great theme that pervaded South Africa's first decade after the fall of apartheid and the election of Nelson Mandela as the country's President and global icon was 'reconciliation'. That theme of reconciliation was perhaps best captured in the spirit of *ubuntu*, which was popularized by Archbishop Desmond Tutu, who headed the country's Truth and Reconciliation Commission (TRC) (see Verdoolaege, this volume; Wilson 2000, 2001; Ross 2002). But *ubuntu* was best embodied by Mandela himself.

Ubuntu is a concept that is difficult to translate into English. Stemming from both the Xhosa and Zulu languages, *ubuntu* comes from the root of the word for 'people' or 'person'. Tutu explains that *ubuntu* is 'the essence of being a person. And in our experience, in our understanding, a person is a person through other persons. You can't be a solitary human being. It's all linked. We have this communal sense, and because of this deep sense of community, the harmony of the group is a prime attribute' (Jaffrey 1998; see Catsam 2004). Another commentator has defined *ubuntu* as meaning: 'I am because we are. I can only be a person through others' (Mbigi 2002: 20).

Whatever the word's interpretations and definitions, it is clearly tied up in concepts of humanity, mutuality, community and compassion. There is a definite communal tone for *ubuntu* that stems from the African tradition in which 'reciprocity, respect for human dignity, social welfare, empathy and solidarity' (Düsing 2002: 297) are vital elements. In this system the individual must subvert self-interest for the sake of the community; or perhaps more accurately, only within the cooperative context of the community can the individual truly find self-interest. One scholar has called *ubuntu* 'a transcendental *geist* of a specifically African nation' (Wilson 1996: 12).

Nelson Mandela's life and career embody the spirit of *ubuntu*. He has often quoted the Xhosa proverb from which the concept is derived, 'Umuntu ngumuntu ngabuntu', which can be translated as, 'a person is a person because of other people' (Sampson 1999: 12). Perhaps no single example of this spirit of reconciliation, of trying to integrate all into the larger community, stands larger than Mandela's willingness to embrace the country's national rugby team, the Springboks. Long a symbol of Afrikaner nationalism and thus of the onerous system of white supremacy that was apartheid, the Springboks were hated by the country's masses, most of whom embraced soccer as their preferred sport and loathed the Springboks, the culture they represented, and the sport they played.[1]

With few exceptions South Africa had become ostracized from the sporting community as the result of the increasing ruthlessness of the enforcers of apartheid. The March 1960 Sharpeville Massacre in which the South African Police (SAP) killed dozens of unarmed protesters and wounded scores more, the majority from being shot in the sides and back as they fled in terror, helped to create the conditions for the sporting boycott that saw South

Africa excluded from the Olympics, the football World Cup, global cricket and nearly all other international sporting events. Occasionally the Springboks would tour abroad, facing teams in New Zealand, Australia and elsewhere, but as the 1970s and 1980s progressed, massive protests met the Springboks wherever they played. Sporting authorities and rugby bosses in the countries that hosted the Springboks tried to claim that sport and politics should never mix, a patently absurd assertion given the intermingling between sports and politics for nearly as long as the two have existed (see MacLean 2003).

Nelson Mandela, a former boxer, was well aware of the power of sport (see Sampson 1999: 516). He also knew that the exclusion of the Springboks from the legitimate sporting community particularly stung white South Africans, especially the Afrikaners for whom rugby was seemingly a life-sustaining source. Once South Africa was on the path to bringing apartheid to an end, the sporting world welcomed the sports-mad country back into the fold. The International Rugby Board (IRB) awarded the country hosting duties for the third Rugby World Cup, a quadrennial event that though new had already firmly established itself as the most important event in rugby's constellation. South Africa's Springboks would once again be allowed to compete against the talented Australians (winners of the 1991 World Cup and thus defending World Champions in 1995); the mighty All Blacks of New Zealand (the 1987 winners who are largely hailed as the sport's dominant force); the English (founders of the game); and the rest of the game's elite teams.

White South Africans were thrilled. But white South Africans have always been a minority in the country. The majority remained largely apathetic, and even hostile. Those rugby fans from the so-called 'black' and 'coloured' communities – and there were always pockets of fans and players across the country – supported anyone but the Springboks in international rugby, and enjoyed watching the national team struggle against opponents who had proven themselves in the crucible of test rugby.

Invictus

It is the run-up and events of this defining moment in South African rugby that are the subject of *Invictus* (2009). The film's director, Clint Eastwood, who has taken on concepts of revenge, forgiveness and reconciliation as *leitmotifs*, especially in the autumn of his long career as an actor and filmmaker, uses this backdrop to depict the merging of rugby and politics as a force for reconciliation in the still-fragile early years of the post-apartheid era.[2] Eastwood portrays Mandela's political savvy but also his sincere embrace of the Springboks during the 1995 World Cup, in which the Springboks made an improbable run to world championship victory.

Invictus opens on the day of Mandela's release from imprisonment on 11 February 1990. Early on Mandela recognizes that he must reconcile with white South Africans and the film reveals him doing so in ways large and small, but the greatest is his strategic embrace of the country's Springbok rugby team as they prepare for the 1995 World Cup, which South Africa is to host. Mandela reaches out to the Springbok captain, Francois Pienaar (played by Matt Damon) who is receptive to the new President's outreach. Not all of his teammates are convinced. The film explores the way Mandela uses rugby to bring about reconciliation and the way the rugby team serves as a medium for the country to embrace reconciliation.

Eastwood's Mandela is played by the lordly Morgan Freeman. Much was made in the media about Freeman's grasp of Mandela's seemingly inimitable cadences and voice timbre. Freeman makes a game effort at capturing the sound of Mandela. But most importantly, he gets the feel right. It rarely escapes the viewer's consciousness that he is watching Freeman play Mandela, but then few characters are as daunting to play on screen. Mandela is arguably the most famous and lauded man in the world.

To make matters more difficult for any actor trying to capture the essence of 'Madiba', the title of respect by which he is known to millions of South Africans, Mandela's greatness decidedly does not come from his speaking style, which most often is halting and even wooden. Mandela has given great speeches, to be sure, but their greatness came from the force of his words and his moral and political authority, and not from his delivery. And so for Freeman to capture the great man, he needed to do so through force of personality, and not merely through mimicry.

Freeman's Mandela, much like the man himself, is a paragon of dignity. Beyond Freeman's successful embodiment of this dignity, the script demonstrates Mandela's munificence in a number of ways. When his bodyguard, Jason (Tony Kgoroge), refuses to work with the Afrikaner special branch assigned to protect the President, Mandela states, 'The Rainbow Nation starts here, reconciliation starts here ... Forgiveness starts here'. His attitude is contrasted with those around him. Following Mandela's afternoon tea with Pienaar, his daughter is given the line, 'I think he looks like one of the policemen who forced us out of your house when you were in gaol. I don't like you seeing you shake his hand and I'm not the only one'. The script illustrates Mandela's ability to straddle the divide in other ways. Early on it is indicated that Mandela, unlike many of those around him, speaks Afrikaans. He is shown recollecting: 'All of my gaolers were Afrikaners. For twenty-seven years I studied them. I learned their books, their poetry. I had to know my enemy before I could prevail against him ... Our enemy is no longer the Afrikaner. They are our fellow South Africans'. Mandela's knowledge of Afrikaans and Afrikaner culture is contrasted with a later scene where Francois Pienaar hands members of the team copies of the Xhosa hymn and anthem of the ANC, 'Nkosi Sikelel' iAfrika' (which at the time of the 1995 World Cup was joint national anthem with 'Die Stem van Suid-Afrika'). His players scrunch the words up complaining, 'It's their bloody song. Not ours' and, most telling, 'I can't even read it or pronounce the words'. (In reality several of the 1995 Springboks warmly embraced learning the anthem, despite some of the scepticism.)

Anthony Peckham's script also portrays Mandela as stubborn, even wilful. When, early on, he decides that backing the Springboks would make for smart symbolism, he does so at the risk of alienating many of his supporters. Eastwood captures this in a scene in which the national governing body of sport has voted to eliminate the Springbok mascot and colours in hopes of erasing the white supremacist meaning of the country's rugby team. Mandela interrupts the meeting (with rather improbable timing, it must be added) and is able just barely to persuade his 'comrades' (then and now the common title of endearment and respect within the ANC) to change their mind. Mandela's staffers are dumbfounded that he would expend his political capital on an issue so seemingly frivolous and repugnant to his main support base. Brenda, Mandela's Chief of Staff (Adjoa Andoh) says, 'You're wasting your political capital. You're risking your political future as our political leader. At least risk it for something more important than rugby'. With so much to address – a tattered economy and a country still torn asunder from apartheid and the transition from it – rugby seems so frivolous, so inapt to Brenda. But Mandela sees farther and knows better.

The film's script hints at, but does not consider directly, the political calculation behind Mandela's decision to maintain the name and colours, and actively support, the Springboks. When challenged by Brenda for his intervention in the National Sports Council meeting, the script has Mandela explaining that the white minority 'still controls the police, the army, and the economy. If we lose them we cannot address the other issues'. 'So this "rugby" is just a political calculation?' asks Brenda. Mandela hesitates and replies, 'It is a human calculation'. A few scenes later, when the Minister of Sport (Shakes Myeko) tells Mandela that the final will be broadcast live to a billion people around the world, Mandela comments, 'A billion people watching us? This is a great opportunity'. And, when the TV shows a successful Springbok 'rugby clinic' in a township, Mandela observes, 'You see that. That picture is worth any number of speeches'.

The Springboks, seen struggling early on and even embarrassing the team's most ardent supporters, including ex-Springbok players-turned-talking-heads, are led by their unassuming captain Francois Pienaar. Eastwood reminds viewers that Pienaar is an

Afrikaner through occasional glimpses at Pienaar's home life in which his family, and especially his father, are depicted as conservatives hostile to Mandela and the recent transition. Following the release of Mandela, Pienaar's father (Patrick Lyster) exclaims, 'I'm telling you Francois. Look at Angola, look at Mozambique, look at Zimbabwe. Are we next? They're going to take our jobs and drive us into the sea. Just you wait'. It would be difficult to assert that the script suggests that the elder Pienaar is racist, because Eastwood steers clear of addressing racism per se, focusing instead on racism's legacies and the difficulties of reconciliation in the aftermath of apartheid, but one gets the sense that the older man knows and has wielded the racist slur *kaffir* a time or two in his life. (The film is not given to distinctions between South Africa's whites and skimps on many other subtleties, and perhaps understandably so, for as it is the film is more than 130 minutes long; South Africa specialists unwilling to accept the film for what it is or those looking for a nuanced history lesson should look elsewhere.) *Invictus* aims to bring the complexities of post-apartheid South Africa to an audience that knows little about South Africa's history. It would be easy to dismiss such efforts from the perch of academia but in this case surely half a loaf is better than none at all – it is not as if Americans, for example, were clamouring to rush to their local university library to track down details of the negotiated settlement or the 1995 Rugby World Cup.

Freeman's depiction of Mandela has been deservedly praised. But Damon has almost as difficult a task. The Afrikaner accent is not an easy one to pull off over the course of a full film and Damon does about as well as any American actor ever has. He plays Pienaar as a reluctant protagonist, pulled into confidence by the wily Mandela, who grows to understand the symbolic importance of the Springbok cause far more quickly than most of his (occasionally woodenly acted) teammates.

The film manages to avoid, or at least skirt, the worst clichés of the inspirational sports film with the obvious caveat that it tackles a pretty damned inspirational sports topic. Eastwood also makes the generally sound decision not to dumb down or over-explain the rugby scenes. There are a few too many slo-mo shots, too many cartoonish insertions of sound effects during those slo-motion bits, and some of the background music is monstrously treacly. But in general Eastwood lets the universal language of sport speak for itself. Few of the viewers of this film, at least those in the United States, will know a scrum from a maul from a line-out. Most will not understand the reason for the many penalty kicks that make up most of the scoring in the championship game pitting the seemingly indomitable All Blacks with their all-world player, Jonah Lomu (a man by way of comparison built like a linebacker who could sprint like a wide receiver), against an improving Springbok side riding what came to be known across the country as 'Madiba Magic'. Most will not grasp the fine points of the Joel Stransky (the Springboks' fly-half) drop goal in extra time that delivered the most implausible world championship. But sports fans will find the internal logic of the game unassailable even if they have no clue about the fine points of how and why exactly it was that the Springboks emerged victorious over the favoured All Blacks.

Invictus is a fine film, even if not an earth-shattering one. Morgan Freeman's portrayal of Mandela seemed like obvious Oscar bait from the outset and indeed he did receive a 'best actor' Oscar nomination as did Damon for 'best supporting actor'. But as with most films depicting historical events, people probably should not learn their history from *Invictus*, even if huge numbers of people will. It is to this that the next section is devoted.

Historical Overreach

The biggest problem with *Invictus* is the conclusion it reaches: that the 1995 World Cup saved South Africa. But for the film's impetus for that interpretation, perhaps we ought to turn to the film's source material: the journalist John Carlin's widely praised book, *Playing the Enemy: Nelson Mandela and the Game that Made a Nation* (2008), which pretty much (over)states its argument in the subtitle.

Carlin's book is an engaging read – I absorbed it in two large gulps the first time I read it. He chose his subject matter well and did his due diligence with his reportage. Indeed, Carlin was a foreign correspondent in South Africa during the transition era and draws from those experiences and his own work on the ground in the 1990s. It was well reviewed and brought both South African affairs and rugby to an audience that may not have much cared about either, at least in the United States. But just as for a man with a hammer every problem becomes a nail, *Playing the Enemy* sometimes makes it seem that the very fate of South Africa hinged on Mandela's embrace of the Springboks. Madiba's act of symbolism was just that, an act of symbolism, and not necessarily a determining factor in South Africa's political successes. And while symbolism is a vital part of politics, it rarely becomes the sole determinant of history. Mandela's savvy use of sport as a way to convey his reconciliatory spirit might have won trust within the white community, but it did not represent a magic palliative for the very real difficulties the country faced.

The hard work of creating the conditions for reconciliation came in the form of the negotiating process that played out in fits and starts over the course of the late 1980s and up to the 1994 elections.[3] Carlin spends an enormous amount of time addressing this process. Indeed, his book about Mandela and the 1995 Springbok World Cup team is largely a tale about Mandela's final years in prison, the conditions of negotiation and the final resolution that created the conditions for Mandela's great act of conciliation at Ellis Park.

These negotiations were crucial, but myriad authors have covered this terrain. So, while Carlin's treatment will probably go down as among the most read, and gracefully written, it is far from the best. The lack of citations and the scant listing of books that Carlin mentions in his 'Note on Sources' (he mentions a grand total of ten books, including something called *Apartheid: The Lighter Side* (Maclennan 1991), which hardly seems indispensable compared to the myriad books he apparently left unread), lead to the conclusion that Carlin is unaware of the many important books and articles covering precisely the terrain that makes up so much of his own book. Professional historians are often accused of jealousy and turf protection when journalists successfully write books about the past. But the fact remains that many of these same journalists do not know what they do not know when it comes to the work that preceded them. As I look at just one of my own bookshelves I see three dozen or more books on South Africa's transition era alone from scholars and journalists, the existence of which Carlin seems blissfully unaware. At times, *Playing the Enemy* does not even represent old wine in new skins inasmuch as Carlin seems unaware of the existence of the old skins.

Furthermore, the actual rugby in the story occupies a far smaller percentage of the book than one would be led to believe by watching the subsequent film. The Rugby World Cup itself occupies less than a fifth of the book. Francois Pienaar, who plays such an important role in *Invictus* and who was so central for the 1995 Springbok side, manages to appear on only nine pages in *Playing the Enemy*. Without that extensive back story covering Mandela's final years in prison and the transition period, Carlin would have had a nice piece of long-form journalism for *Esquire*, *The New Yorker* or *The Atlantic Monthly* rather than a book. In contrast, Eastwood's *Invictus* wisely focuses predominantly on the rugby element of the book rather than the back story to which Carlin devotes so much space.

Invictus (and ESPN's 30 for 30 series documentary *The 16th Man*, which also relies on Carlin's work), however, does promote Carlin's idea that the 1995 Rugby World Cup did 'make a nation'. Early on the film recreates the first international test match between England and the Springboks at Loftus Versfeld stadium in June 1994 (which South Africa lost 15 to 32). We are shown a group of black South African supporters cheering as England score their first try. A few minutes later Mandela, watching the match, speaks to his personal assistant: 'Look at this. All of the whites are cheering for the Springboks. All of the blacks are cheering for England. We used to do that on the island you know. We would cheer for anyone but the 'Boks. It made the warders very angry'.

Likewise, that black South Africans preferred soccer is emphasized from the start of the film. The first scene takes place on the

165

day of Nelson Mandela's 11 February 1990 release from prison and shows his police convoy passing down a road where on one side well-kitted white pupils practice rugby with their sports master in a well-appointed sports field with a sturdy steel fence, while on the other side of the road black South African kids play soccer on a piece of waste ground surrounded by a flimsy chain-link fence. While the black kids cheer and shout 'Madiba' the white sports master tells his pupils, 'Remember this day boys. This is the day our country went to the dogs'. The animosity of black South Africans towards rugby continues to be illustrated throughout the film. When François Pienaar comes to have tea with Mandela, one of the black bodyguards asks, 'Who is this François Pienaar?' to which his white colleague replies, 'You can't be serious. He's the captain of the Springboks'. 'I like soccer myself', the black bodyguard replies.

By the closing credits, however, we are shown black South Africans playing rugby in a township accompanied by the 1995 World Cup anthem sung by Ladysmith Black Mambazo and P.J. Powers (although the words were originally written for the 1991 World Cup in England) and its final line, 'A new age has begun' (which also rings out when Pienaar raises the World Cup at the end of the final match).

One of the devices the film uses to demonstrate this transformation is a young, black boy from the townships. We first encounter him at a church clothes distribution. Arriving last, a white woman hands him a shirt saying, 'You're a very lucky boy. It's a real Springbok practice jersey'. The boy runs out. The woman asks her black companion why he refused to take it. 'If he wears it,' she replies, 'the others will beat him up'. 'Because the Springboks are playing so badly?' the white woman naively asks. 'No, because for them the Springboks still represent apartheid'. At the climax of the film the same little boy is shown cheering the Springboks as they arrive at the final at Johannesburg's Ellis Park. The transformation is completed by a series of cutaways during the final match. First, the boy cautiously stands by a police car outside the stadium where officers are listening to the match on the car radio (they tell him to go away).

Rugby, Race, Madiba and the *Invictus* Creation Myth

As the tension mounts, a series of cutaways show him sitting on the bonnet listening with the two policeman; then cheering with them as the final whistle blows and extra time begins; then all three drinking Coke that the police have bought; and, with the final whistle and South Africa's victory, the white policemen hoist him on their shoulders, one placing his cap on the boy's head (perhaps mirroring an earlier scene where Francois Pienaar gives Mandela a Springbok cap). The boy's earlier animosity to rugby is replaced with joyous investment; the white police officers' animosity to black South Africans is replaced with sport-induced camaraderie.

There is no doubt that the 1995 World Cup triumph represented a wonderful moment for South Africans, especially for fans of the Springboks, while the willingness of Mandela, and of many Africans, to embrace the team (*Amabokoboko*, Zulu for 'Our Springboks', became something of a catchphrase in 1995 and beyond) 1995 did not mark the magic turning point in the country that these closing scenes imply. The Truth and Reconciliation Commission (TRC), established to deal with the gross human rights violations in South Africa in the period after 1960, and thus to do much of the hard work of addressing the painful apartheid past, had yet to even convene when Stransky's kick sailed into history.[4] And South African rugby was hardly free from politics of racism in the years to follow. The World Cup represented a feel-good moment. But it would be a misreading of history to imply that rugby represented the *sine qua non* of reconciliation in South Africa and it would do a tremendous disservice to the work of thousands of South Africans less heralded than Mandela and Pienaar to suggest that all it took was for Mandela to don the number 6 jersey for all to be well in a country that is still struggling to reconcile its racist history.

To argue that this sports film teaches us a rather facile lesson about South African history does not mean that sport did not play an important role in that history. But, it is important to recognize that the 1995 Springboks, and the history of rugby in South Africa generally, represents but one example of this role (as the next section will illustrate with the case of Robben Island). But for the mass of South Africans rugby was not the sport of choice. Chester Williams, the team's sole black player helped to bridge the racial divide, and Eastwoood uses a scene with the Springboks reluctantly going to give a clinic to black children to show how Williams served the Springboks well as a symbol of the New South Africa and rugby's potential role within it. But one can easily imagine that when the euphoria faded, those children tossed aside the peculiarly shaped rugby ball and resumed their own preferred game: a game Americans know as 'soccer'. Furthermore, the film does not acknowledge that under apartheid, Williams was designated as 'coloured', rather than 'African', and his native tongue is Afrikaans – details that complicate the simple tale of the sole 'black' Springbok on the 1995 side.[5]

Fighting Apartheid through Sport

Black South Africans may not have embraced rugby in the same way that their white counterparts did, but long before Mandela saw the wisdom in pulling the country behind *Amabokoboko* black South Africans had leveraged sport for political gain. And one of the places where they had done so was most unlikely.

Robben Island is perhaps the most notorious prison in world history. Located four miles off the coast of Cape Town, in forbidding waters, Robben Island served as a symbol of apartheid's power and ruthlessness. Mandela famously spent the bulk of his twenty-seven years in state custody on the island where privation was the norm and where the capriciousness of the prison guards was matched only by their penchant for cruelty.

It is in references to Robben Island that the significance of the film's title is gradually revealed. When Pienaar firsts goes for tea with the President, Mandela tells him, 'On Robben Island, when things got very bad, I found inspiration in ... a Victorian poem' (see Daniels 1998: 244). Later we are shown Mandela writing out *Invictus* (a poem by the English poet William Ernest Henley) on presidential note paper which, on the day before South Africa's opening World Cup match against Australia, Mandela hands to

Pienaar, explaining, 'I have something for you. It has helped me through the years, I hope it helps you'. Finally, in a scene where Pienaar and his team take a break from training to visit Robben Island, Pienaar stands in Mandela's former cell where a ghostly Mandela first appears breaking rocks outside and then reading *Invictus* inside.

But to reduce the tale of Robben Island to one of brutality, as these scenes do, is to miss out on a more important sporting story. For even amidst Robben Island's tragedy emerged hope, optimism, and resilience. It was at the island prison that 'Robben Island University', which some refer to as 'Mandela University,' emerged. Generations of anti-apartheid leaders, already committed to the cause, as evidenced by their imprisonment, earned virtual graduate educations in protest and resistance there. Many earned formal educational credentials via correspondence courses.

Even more important is the role that sport itself played at Robben Island. At Robben Island the political prisoners demanded the ability to play sports. What at first seemed little more than folly ultimately resulted in Robben Island's development of a comprehensive sports programme with multiple competitive leagues. The crown jewel of this sporting subculture was soccer, and for all involved maintaining a successful, competitive soccer programme was the priority. But once soccer was established the prisoners began to push for other sports, including even rugby, which was alien to most of the prisoners and which at first met with overt hostility from many who associated the game with the worst elements of apartheid.

It is this story of sport on Robben Island that American historian Chuck Korr and British writer Marvin Close explore in their fine book *More Than Just a Game: Football v Apartheid* (2008). From the outset Korr and Close make it clear that the desire to organize sport at the prison island was never about sport per se. To be sure, the prisoners wanted the exercise, the competition, the camaraderie, and the fleeting freedom that sport would offer. But they also saw sport as a path to some independence, to organization, to leadership and to freedom not only fleeting but real.

Korr and Close meticulously recount the way in which organizing football leagues became a pastime that could be all-consuming. But it also revealed the discipline that the prisoners were capable of mustering. When prison authorities refused to make concessions that the players and officials thought were essential, they would refuse to play. What at first blush seemed to be self-flagellating and thus self-defeating, instead revealed the men to be deeply committed to principles more than to mere play.

And while sports represented politics by other means for the prisoners against the authorities, they often also revealed the many complicated political differences among the prisoners. Organizing sport also forced the players, referees and officials to work with one another in ways that might never have otherwise happened. Sport bridged gaps between the prisoners and the prison officials, but it also bridged the chasms between prisoners. In a very real way the effort to bring play to Robben Island both drew from the experiences fighting apartheid on the mainland and fuelled their ability to organize and ultimately lead the country after the 1994 elections.

Conclusion

These are good days for South African sport in many ways. The 2009 Springboks were inarguably the best team in the world. The Proteas, the national cricket team, continue to be one of the best national sides (though they also continue to disappoint on the biggest stages). And while Bafana Bafana, the national soccer team, has not played especially well in recent years, the country successfully hosted the 2010 World Cup, the globe's biggest sporting event and the most significant event ever to come to South Africa, indeed to Africa. The World Cup proved to be an event every bit as symbolically resonant as the 1995 World Cup, and perhaps more so since the country's embrace of the event ran far deeper.

But politics, race and nationalism will continue to intertwine in South Africa. They are, indeed, inextricably mixed. More black players than ever play in the Springbok team; some are among the best players in the world and are loved by 'Bok fans black and white. Yet the legacy of racism continues to haunt the sport, and as a result some still would like to see the removal of the Springbok mascot. Soccer is still an overwhelmingly black sport, and the fear across the country is that white soccer fans do not care about either the country's professional soccer league or, outside of the nation-building boost of the World Cup, Bafana Bafana, preferring instead to follow the English Premier League and to root for international teams such as England or the Netherlands. Yet among black fans, in recent years arguably the most popular member of the national team is Matthew Booth, a tall white defender with a shaved head upon whom the fans shower adoring calls of 'Booooooooth' every time he touches the ball (cries that have confused visiting European media members in the past who confused calling out Booth's name with catcalls and thus racism against the team's sole white player) (see Catsam 2010b).

The 2010 football World Cup mobilized South Africans, black, white, Indian, and 'coloured', in celebration of their country and their continent. Because of his own frail health and a death in his family Mandela's literal presence at the World Cup was sadly limited even as his metaphorical presence provided the backdrop for the entire event. But for all of the glories of the World Cup there is still poverty and unemployment and millions of South Africans will be unlikely to see the benefits of the world's grandest sporting events.

Sport in South Africa, like the country itself, is profoundly complicated. There is no need for simplified narratives of redemption. The reality is fascinating enough.

Notes

1. On rugby, race, nationalism and politics see Catsam (2010a, 2010b), Naughright (1997: 76–100), Black and Naughright (1998) and Grundlingh et al. (1995).
2. There are myriad examples of Eastwood's commitment to themes of forgiveness and redemption, most prominent among them *Gran Torino* (2008) and *Unforgiven* (1992).

3. A sample of the vast literature includes Waldemir (1997), Sparks (1995), Harvey (2001) and Davenport (1998).
4. The literature on the TRC is vast and continues to grow. In addition to my work cited above, the best starting point is a series of massive bibliographies on the TRC (see Institute for Justice and Reconciliation 2001; Alexander et al. 2004; Doxtader 2010).
5. It is worth noting that *Safundi: The Journal of South African and American Studies* held a roundtable on *Invictus* in Volume 13 Issues 1–2 pp. 115–51.

Filmography

Eastwood, C. (Dir.) 1992. *Unforgiven* (Warner Bros, Malpaso Productions).

Eastwood, C. (Dir.) 2008. *Gran Torino* (Matten Productions, Double Nickel Entertainment, Gerber Pictures, Malpaso Productions, Media Magik Entertainment, Village Roadshow Pictures, WV Films IV, Warner Bros. Pictures).

Eastwood, C. (Dir.) 2009. *Invictus* (Warner Bros. Pictures, Spyglass Entertainment, Revelations Entertainment, Malpaso Productions).

Bestall, C. (Dir.) 2010. *The 16th Man* (ESPN Films 30 for 30).

References

Alexander, K., D. Batchelor, A. Durand and T. Savage. 2004. 'Truth Commissions and Transitional Justice: Update on a Select Bibliography on the South African Truth and Reconciliation Debate', *Journal of Law and Religion* 20(2): 525–65.

Black, D.R. and J. Naughright. 1998. *Rugby and the South African Nation: Sport, Culture, Politics and Power in the Old and New South Africas*. Manchester: Manchester University Press.

Carlin, J. 2008. *Playing the Enemy: Nelson Mandela and the Game that Made a Nation*. London: Atlantic.

Catsam, D. 2004. 'Text, Lies, and Videotape: Truth, Reconciliation, and Transition to Democracy in the New South Africa', *Proteus: A Journal of Ideas* 21(1): 13–22.

———. 2010a. 'Stopped at the Try Line?: Rugby, Race, and Nationalism in the New South Africa', *Impumelelo: The Interdisciplinary Electronic Journal of African Sport* 5(2010). Retrieved 1 November 2011 from http://www.ohio.edu/sportsafrica/journal/volume5/castman.htm

_____. 2010b. 'The Death of Doubt'. *Sport, Race, and Nationalism in the New South Africa*', *Georgetown Journal of International Affairs* 11(2), pp. 7–13.

Daniels, E. 1998. *There and Back: Robben Island, 1964–1979*. Cape Town: Mayibuye Books.

Davenport, T. 1998. *The Birth of a New South Africa*, Toronto: University of Toronto Press.

Doxtader, E. (ed.). 2010. 'The South African Truth and Reconciliation Commission: A Bibliography of Recent Works'. Retrieved 1 November 2011 from http://www.scribd.com/doc/54276261/Truth-and-Reconciliation-Commission-Bibliography-3-2

Düsing, S. 2002. *Traditional Leadership and Democratisation in Southern Africa: A Comparative Study of Botswana, Namibia, and Southern Africa*. Munster: Lit Verlag.

Grundlingh, A., A. Odendaal and B. Spies. 1995. *Beyond the Tryline: Rugby and South African Society*. Johannesburg: Ravan Press.

Grundlingh, A., S. Robolin, A. Hinsman, L. Saint, S. Pearl and S. Pinto. 2012. 'Roundtable on *Invictus*', *Safundi: The Journal of South African and American Studies*, 13(1&2): 115–51.

Harvey, R. 2001. *The Fall of Apartheid: The Inside Story From Smuts to Mbeki*. New York: Palgrave MacMillan.

Institute for Justice and Reconciliation. 2001. 'Truth Commissions and Transitional Justice: A Select Bibliography on the South African Truth and Reconciliation Debate', *Journal of Law and Religion* 16(1): 69–186.

Jaffrey, Z. 1998. 'Interview with Desmond Tutu – chair of South Africa's Truth and Reconciliation Commission', *The Progressive*, 2 February.

Korr, C.P. and M. Close. 2008. *More than Just a Game: Football v Apartheid*. London: Collins.

MacLean, M. 2003. 'Making Strange the Country and Making Strange the Countryside: Spatialized Clashes in the Affective Economies of Aotearoa/New Zealand during the 1981 Springbok Rugby Tour', in John Bale and Mike Cronin (eds), *Sport and Postcolonialism*. Oxford: Berg, pp. 57–72.

Maclennan, B. 1991. *Apartheid: The Lighter Side*. Cape Town: Chameleon Press in association with the Carrefour Press.

Mbigi, L. 2002. 'Spirit of African Leadership: A Comparative African Perspective', *Journal for Convergence* 3(4): 18–23.

Naughright, J. 1997. *Sport, Cultures and Identities in South Africa*. David Philip: Cape Town.

Ross, F.C. 2002. *Bearing Witness: Women and the Truth and Reconciliation Commission in South Africa*. London: Pluto Press.

Sampson, A. 1999. *Mandela: The Authorized Biography*. New York: Alfred A. Knopf.

Sparks, A. 1995. *Tomorrow Is Another Country: The Inside Story of South Africa's Road to Change*. Chicago: University of Chicago Press.

Waldmeir, P. 1997. *Anatomy of a Miracle: The End of Apartheid and the Birth of the New South Africa* New York: Norton.

Wilson, R. 1996. 'The Sizwe Will Not Go Away. The Truth and Reconciliation Commission, Human Rights and Nation-Building in South Africa', *African Studies* 55(2): 1–20.

_____. 2000. 'Reconciliation and Revenge in Post-Apartheid South Africa: Rethinking Legal Pluralism and Human Rights', *Current Anthropology* 41(1): 75–98.

_____. 2001. *The Politics of Truth and Reconciliation in South Africa: Legitimizing the Post-Apartheid State*. Cambridge: Cambridge University Press.

Notes on Contributors

Daniel Branch is Associate Professor of African History at the University of Warwick. He is the author of *Defeating Mau Mau, Creating Kenya: Counterinsurgency, Civil War and Decolonization* (Cambridge University Press, 2009) and *Kenya: Between Hope and Despair, 1963–2011* (Yale University Press, 2011). He is co-editor of *Our Turn to Eat: Politics in Kenya since 1950* (Lit Verlag, 2010).

Derek Charles Catsam is Associate Professor of history at the University of Texas of the Permian Basin. He is the author of *Freedom's Main Line: the Journey of Reconciliation and the Freedom Rides* (University Press of Kentucky, 2009) and *Bleeding Red: A Red Sox Fan's Diary of the 2004 Season* (New Academia, 2005). He is currently working on a monograph on bus boycotts in the United States and South Africa in the 1940s and 1950s.

Nigel Eltringham is Senior Lecturer in Social Anthropology at the University of Sussex. He is the author of *Accounting for Horror: Post-Genocide Debates in Rwanda* (Pluto, 2004). He is currently working on a monograph on the International Criminal Tribunal for Rwanda and an edited collection entitled *Remembering Genocide* (Routledge, forthcoming).

Danny Hoffman is Associate Professor of Anthropology and Director of the African Studies Program at the University of Washington. He is the author of *The War Machines: Young Men and Violence in Sierra Leone and Liberia* (Duke University Press, 2011). In addition to his ethnographic research, Hoffman worked as a photojournalist in Africa and the Balkans.

Notes on Contributors

Lidwien Kapteijns is Professor of African and Middle Eastern History at Wellesley College. She is the author of *Women's Voices in a Man's World: Women and the Pastoral Tradition in Northern Somali Orature, c. 1899–1980* (Heinemann, 1999) and *Clan Cleansing in Somalia: The Ruinous Legacy of 1991* (University of Pennsylvania Press, 2012). She is contributing co-editor of *African Mediations of Violence: Fashioning New Futures from Contested Pasts* (Brill, 2010).

Mark Leopold is Lecturer in Social Anthropology at the University of Sussex. He is the author of *Inside West Nile: Violence, History and Representation on an African Frontier* (James Currey, 2005), and has published a number of journal articles and edited book chapters on conflict and violence in North East Africa. He is currently working on a biography of Idi Amin for Yale University Press.

Annelies Verdoolaege is Postdoctoral Researcher in the Department of African Languages and Cultures at Ghent University. She has published in the fields of discourse analysis, political sciences and cultural studies, and on various aspects of the South African Truth and Reconciliation Commission. She is the author of *Reconciliation Discourse: The Case of the Truth and Reconciliation Commission* (John Benjamins, 2008).

Index

accuracy, 40, 51, 60, 118–21
Achebe, Chinua, 5
Afghanistan, 39, 62, 63, 64, 65, 66
Africa
  as category, 5–14, 108–9
  composite, 7–8
African National Congress (ANC),
  136, 137–8, 141, 153n6–7
African Queen, The, 2
African Studies Association 1
Aidiid, Mohamed Farah, 46, 48,
  49, 50, 52, 53, 60, 64, 66, 67n13,
  68n20
Akulia, Margaret, 28–29
Algeria, 3
al-Qaeda, 63–64, 65
Allen, Sir Peter, 31
Amabokoboko, 167, 168
Amin, Idi, 13, 14, 21–36, 36n13,
  37n15
  as patriot, 32–35
  and Scotland, 29–32
Amin, Jaffar, 28–29, 37n17
Amin, Kay, 25
Amin, Taban, 28, 37n16
Andrew, Dudley, 108
Anker, D.: 'Imaginary Witness',
  130n5
apartheid, 2, 135, 136–37, 140, 141,
  148, 157, 166, 167, 168
  and betrayal, 145–48
Armed Forces Revolutionary Council
  (AFRC; Sierra Leone), 94, 110n4
Arusha Accords, 120, 121
Askari, 146, 153n6

Astles, Bob, 25, 36n9
Atlantic Monthly (journal), 98
Ato, Osman Ali, 52, 53, 67–68n18–19
Attenborough, Richard, 12
Azanian People's Liberation Army,
  150

Babel, 3
Bafana Bafana soccer team, 170, 171
Barre, Mohamed Siyad, 42, 47
BBC, 8, 9, 10, 105, 113, 114, 118–19,
  120–21
Beata, 116
Belton, David, 113, 114, 118, 124
Benzien, Jeffrey, 14, 144, 146, 152
Beyond the Gates. See *Shooting Dogs*
Black Hawk Down, 2, 8, 9, 10, 39–66,
  106
  depiction of Somalis 8, 9, 10, 40,
    41–42, 52–57, 64, 65–66, 68n20,
    68n23, 68n28
  depiction of US forces, 41, 50–52,
    57–58
  DVD, 66
  framing, 40, 46–50
  'legends' 62
  summary, 41–42
  truth claims, 43–46
  shown as victory, 59–66
  video game, 68n22
  Washington screening, 61–62
'Black Hawk Down' (poem), 68n31
Blood Diamond, 2, 6, 7, 8, 9, 10, 11,
  91–109, 110n11
  crime in country, 102–5

Index

DVD version, 109n1
and Sierra Leone war, 93–95
urban/rural relationships, 95–102
war in the city, 105–9
Blumenthal, S., 47
Bolger, D.P., 67n9, 67n15, 69n31
Booth, Matthew, 171
Born Free, 2
Bosnia, 7, 10
Bourne Ultimatum, The, 3
Boutros-Ghali, 49
Bowden, Mark: *Black Hawk Down*, 39, 44, 45, 50–51, 52, 54, 55–56, 57, 63, 64–55, 68n28–30
Branch, Daniel, 14, 175
Bruckheimer, Jerry, 39, 43, 51, 55, 61, 63
Buko Pharma-Kampagne, 85, 87n10
Burlas, Joe, 61
Bush, George, 46–47, 48, 65, 82
Bush, George W., 61–62
Busharizi, Paul, 24

Caine, Jeffrey, 72
Cameron, Kenneth, 14
Camp de Tharoye, 12
Campbell, Greg, 101
Campbell, Naomi, 110n9
CARE, 48
Carlin, John: *Playing the Enemy*, 163–65
Carr, E.H., 12
Caton-Jones, Michael, 11, 116, 124, 130
Catsam, Derek, 12, 13, 175
Chrisman, Laura, 105, 110n6
City of God, 73
Civil Defence Force (Sierra Leone), 100–101
Clinton, Bill, 46, 62, 65
Clockwork Orange, 92
Close, Marvin, 169–70
Collier, Paul, 100

colonialism, 2, 3, 5, 32–33
Conrad, Joseph: *Heart of Darkness*, 24
Conspiracy, 116–17
Constant Gardener, The, 2, 4, 6, 10–11, 12, 14, 72–80, 81, 83–86
Constant Gardener Trust, 85, 87n11
Crane, David, 100–101, 110n10
Cry Freedom, 2, 12
Cry Freetown, 106
Curic, Vjeko, 118–19

Dallaire, Romeo, 114, 118, 119
Damon, Matt, 159, 162, 163
Darfur, 2
Delta Force (video game), 68n22
Deme, Amadou, 118, 119
diamond trade, 6, 94–5, 99–100, 101, 103, 104–5, 106, 110n9
Dowd, William J., 54
drugs, pharmaceutical, 6, 73–77, 78, 84, 85–86
Dry White Season, A, 2
Duage-Roth, Alexandre, 121
Durant, Mike, 52, 53–54, 60, 62, 66, 68n20, 68n27

Eastwood, Clint, 159, 161, 162–63, 165, 168, 171n2
ECOMOG, 110n11
Economist, The (journal), 92, 109n2
Eltringham, Nigel, 175
'Besieged history?', 130n1
empathy, 10–11, 51–52, 123–27
Essence of Combat, The, 44
Ethiopia, 42, 48

Fanon, Frantz, 104
Feldman, Allen, 115
Firimbi, Abdullah Hassan, 52, 53–54
First, Ruth, 152
Foden, Giles: *The Last King of Scotland*, 21, 24, 25, 27, 35

Index

Fort Benning, Georgia, 43
Fourie, Ginn, 150
framing, 40, 46–50
France, 3
Fransch, Anton, 146
Freeman, Morgan, 159–60, 163
Freetown, Sierra Leone, 91–92, 94–96, 101, 102, 103, 105–8, 109
Fullard, M., 143

Gberie, L., 109n3
General, Idi Amin Dada A Self-portrait, 22, 27, 34, 35–36, 36n13
genocide, 7, 9, 113, 114, 115–16, 118–26, 128–30
geo-conflation, 7, 118
geo-politics, 5
George, Terry, 1, 4, 113, 115, 122, 128, 130
Githongo, John, 79–80
globalization, 82–83, 85–86
Goodbye Bafana, 2
Gouri, Haim, 130n4
Grahame, Major Iain, 25
Gran Torino, 171n2
Gulf War, 47, 48

Halbwachs, Maurice, 128
Hanna, 3
Hatari!, 2
Hawk, Beverley, 6, 7
Henley, William Ernest: 'Invictus', 168
Henry, Yazir, 146
heroism, 3, 4, 11, 51–52, 59
Hirsch, Joshua, 122, 125
history, written, 12–13, 115–16
Hobsbawm, Eric, 82
Hoeffler, Anke, 100
Hoffman, Danny, 9, 175
Hollywood, 40, 43, 92, 108, 109
Holocaust, 115, 116, 121, 122, 127–28, 130, 130n4

Holocaust (TV series), 113, 123
Holt, J.D.F., 37n21
Hommes et des Dieux, Des, 3
Hors-la-loi, 3
Hotel Rwanda, 1, 4, 6, 7, 8, 9, 10, 113–14, 115–19, 121–30
 accuracy, 118–21
 DVD, 122–23
 empathy, 123–27
Hughes, Nick: *The Hunger Business*, 121–22, 130n3
Huyssen, Andreas, 123

I Dreamed of Africa, 86
imperialism, 7
Indigènes, 3
In My Country, 2
International Rugby Board, 158
Invictus, 2, 9, 12, 13, 159–63, 165–69
Iseta: Behind the Roadblock, 130n3
Israel, 36n2, 36n9, 37n19
Iweala, Uzodinma: *Beasts of No Nation*, 99, 110n8

Jackson, Michael, 125
Journal of Public Health Policy, 75
Judt, Tony, 85

Kabuye, K., 36n3
Kagame, Paul, 128–29
Kalyegira, Timothy, 32–33
Kampala, 26
Kano state, 76–77
Kaplan, Robert: 'The Coming Anarchy', 98, 99, 108; *The Coming Anarchy*, 82–83
Kapteijns, Lidwien, 10, 67n8, 67n12, 176
Keane, John M., 61
Keen, D., 109–10n3
Kenya, 14, 64, 73–74, 77–81, 84–85
 health care, 77–81

179

Index

Kenya African National Union (KANU), 79
Kenyatta, Jomo, 79, 80
Khartoum, 2
Kibaki, Mwai, 79–80
Kigali, 114, 116, 119, 128
King's African Rifles (KAR), 25, 28, 36n14
Klein, Naomi, 82
Kock, Eugene de, 148, 149, 152
Kono, 94, 104
Korr, Chuck, 169–70
Krio, 96, 110n7
Krog, A., 146
Kyemba, Henry: *State of Blood*, 27–28

Lacy, Mark, 40, 50–51, 59, 66, 69n31
Last King of Scotland, The, 2, 4–5, 9, 11, 13, 14, 21–29, 32, 33–35
Last Safari, The, 2
Lawrence, J.S., 57, 59–60, 61, 67n5, 67n7,
le Carré, John, 4, 72–73
  The Constant Gardener, 4, 72–73, 74, 81–82, 83–84
  The Secret Pilgrim, 72
Leopold, Mark, 3, 4–5, 11, 13, 176
Liberia, 93, 94, 110n9
Lisle, D., 45, 67n2–4
Lord of War, 2
Lugard, Frederick, 1st Baron, 28
Lumet, Sidney, 114
Lund, Kátia, 73
Lustig, Branko, 68n24

Macdonald, Kevin, 21, 22, 24, 25, 26–27, 29, 34
Malkki, Liisa, 15n3
Mandela, Nelson, 157, 171
  portrayed in film, 159–62, 163
  President, 139, 156
  release, 9, 137, 166
  and sport, 158, 159, 160–61, 163–65, 167, 168
  in state custody, 165, 168–69
Mangold, Tom, 29–30
Man Who Shot Liberty Valance, The, 21
mapping, 5
Max, Arthur, 68n24
Mazrui, Ali, 34
Mbalu-Mukasa, 25
McGarrahan, J.G., 57, 59–60, 61, 67n5, 67n7
Meirelles, Fernando, 73, 85
Melvern, Linda, 119
Membe, Achille, 5, 11
Mende, 94, 110n5
Merck, 74–75, 86n2
Mission for Essential Drugs and Supplies, 80–81, 86n8
Mo'allim, Yusuf Dahir, 52, 53
Mogadishu, 39, 43, 55, 57, 59, 60, 62, 63, 67n15, 68n28
Mogambo, 2
Moi, Daniel arap, 79
Monitor, The (Ugandan newspaper), 32
Morocco, 3, 7, 39, 44, 54, 55
Mozambique, 102, 109
Mudimbe, V.Y., 5
Mukiibi, Abbey, 24
Munich Olympics, 36n2
Museveni, Yoweri, 23–24, 28, 36n7
music, 58
myth, 35, 40, 50–59

Nagenda, John, 24, 33, 36n4–5, 37n24
National Rainbow Coalition, 79
necklacing, 146, 153n7
Nelson, Shawn, 55–56
New Times, The (Rwandan newspaper), 129

Index

New Vision (newspaper), 33, 36n3–8, 36n10, 37n16, 37n22–23
news media, 6–10, 105–6
Ngugi, Catherine Njieri, 12
Nigeria, 76–77, 86n3–4, 110n11
Nolan, Ken, 39, 68n24, 68n26
Novartis, 75

Oakley, Robert, 49, 60, 67n12, 67n14, 68n19–20
Obote, Milton, 36n9
One Day in September, 36n2
Operation Gothic Serpent (U.S.), 67n15
Operation Irene (U.S.), 39, 41–42, 43, 45–46, 48–50, 51, 57, 59–60, 61–62, 68n20–21
Operation Restore Hope (U.S.), 48
orientalism, 5–6, 8–9
Osama bin Laden, 63–64
Out of Africa, 2, 85, 86n1
Oxfam, 75

Pawnbroker, The, 114–15, 127–28
Pearson, Keir, 113
Peckham, Anthony, 160
Pepper, A., 45, 67n2–4
Pfizer, 76, 77, 86n3–4
pharmaceutical companies, 6, 73–77, 78, 84, 85–86
Pienaar, Francois, 159, 161–62, 165, 166, 167, 168–69
Pierpaoli, Yvette, 85
Poggiolini, Diulio, 86
Pollack, Sydney, 85
Powell, Colin, 47
Prospect (magazine), 33, 37n24
Proteas cricket team, 170

realism, 11, 12, 60, 122
Red Dust, 2, 9, 15n4, 135–36, 138, 141–53
betrayal, 145–48

forgiveness, 148–50
setting, 141–42
torture, 14, 136, 142–45
refugees, 15n3, 48
restorative justice, 140–41
Revolutionary United Front (RUF; Sierra Leone), 93–94, 96, 97, 100, 102–8, 110n3–4
Robben Island, 168–70
Robbins, Anthony, 75
Rorty, Richard, 123–24, 126, 127
Rosentsone, Robert, 13, 119
Rouche, Jean, 34
Rousseau, N., 143
Ruiz, Sgt., 62
Rusesabagina, Paul, 114, 124, 128–29
Rusesabagina, Tatiana, 114, 128
Rutaganda, Georges, 118
Rwanda, 7, 113, 114–30, 130n6
Rwandan Patriotic Front (RPF), 120, 121

Safari, 73
Safundi (journal), 172n5
Said, Edward, 5–6, 7, 8–9, 12
Sankoh, Foday, 94
Schroeder, Barbet, 22, 27, 32, 34–35
Scotland, 29–31
Scott, Ridley, 39, 43, 44–45, 46, 51, 55, 61, 63, 64–65
Scottish nationalists, 30–31
Sembène, Ousame, 12
Sharpeville Massacre, 157
Shelley, Christine, 121
Shooting Dogs, 2, 6, 8, 9, 10, 11, 113, 114, 115–21, 123–28, 130
Sierra Leone, 7, 91, 109
Army, 93, 97, 110n4, 110n11
Special Court for, 100–1, 110n9–10
war, 92, 93–109
see also Freetown
Simba, 73
16th Man, The, 165

181

Index

Slovo, Gillian: *Red Dust*, 152
Smuts, Jan, 136
Snows of Kilimanjaro, The, 2
Somali Republic, 42
Somalia, 7, 39–66, 67n11–13, 68n20
　history, 41–42
　Somalis, film depiction of, 8, 9, 10, 40, 41–42, 52–57, 64, 65–66, 68n20, 68n23, 68n28 and U.S., 43–50
Something of Value, 73
Sometimes in April, 2
Somora, Sorious, 106
South Africa, 2, 7, 13, 14, 135–53
　apartheid, 2, 135, 136–37, 140, 141, 148, 157, 166, 167, 168
　national reconciliation, 149, 150, 156, 157, 164
　sport, 157–71
South African Truth and Reconciliation Commission (TRC), 9, 14, 135, 136–37, 138–41, 148, 149–50, 151–52, 153, 153n2, 156, 167
　Amnesty Committee, 135, 136, 138–39, 143–44, 146–47, 148, 150, 152
　Committee on Reparation and Rehabilitation, 139–40
　Human Rights Violation Committee, 138, 142–43, 145–46
　Investigation Unit, 149
　literature on, 172n4
　women, 151–52
　sport, 157–71
　on Robben Island, 169–70
Springboks, 157–63, 164, 165–68, 170–71
Springer, Claudia, 45
Struecker, Jeff, 60–61
Sudan, 64
Sunday Monitor (Ugandan newspaper), 34, 37n25

Tanzania, 137
Taylor, Charles, 93, 110n9
Tears of the Sun, 2
Togane, Mohamud S.: poem by, 66, 68n31
torture, 14, 136, 142–45
Transparency International, 78–79
Trovan, 76–77
Tutu, Desmond, Archbishop, 156–57

Uganda, 4–5, 13, 21–29, 31–35, 36n1, 36n9, 36n13, 37n15
unbutu, 156–57
Unforgiven, 171n2
Unified Task Force (U.N./U.S.), 67n11
United Nations (U.N.), 49, 50, 54, 110n9
　Human Development Index, 78, 86n7
　peacekeepers, 94
　UNAMIR, 114, 118, 119, 120–21
　UNHCR, 48
　UNOSOM II, 49, 52, 67n11
United States (U.S.)
　military, 39, 40–66
　Department of the Army Urban Operations manual, 98–99
　Marines, 48
　Task Force Ranger (TFR), 41–42, 43–44, 46, 48–49, 50, 51–53, 58–62, 67n1, 67n11
　USAID, 47–48
urbanization, 97–99
Uwilingiyimana, Agathe, 120

Valmajo, Joaquín, 118
Verdoolaege, Annelies, 14, 176
Vietnam, 47
Vlakplaas farm, Sierra Leone, 148
Voice of America, 130n6

Waal, A. de, 49, 67n13
Waldorf, Lars, 129

Index

Walkowitz, Daniel, 118
Wannsee conference, 116–17
Ward, Julie, 77
Washington Post, 76–77
Weiss, Peter: *The Investigation*, 115
Whitaker, Forest, 22, 25, 26, 27, 33–34, 36, 37n17, 37n23
White Mischief, 2, 86n1
Wiesel, Elie, 113–14, 115, 117, 123, 129, 130
Williams, Chester, 168

World Food Organization, 48
Wrong, Michela, 126

Yengeni, Tony, 144
Young, Crawford, 84
Yugoslavia, 127

Zimmer, Hans, 58
Zulu, 2
Zwick, Edward, 9, 91–92, 102, 103, 106, 108, 109n1, 110n11